Infectious
Mononucleosis

Titles in the Diseases and Disorders series include:

DISEASES & DISORDERS

Infectious Mononucleosis

Hal Marcovitz

LUCENT BOOKS
A part of Gale, Cengage Learning

GALE
CENGAGE Learning

Detroit • New York • San Francisco • New Haven, Conn • Waterville, Maine • London

GALE
CENGAGE Learning™

LIBRARY OF CONGRESS CATALOGING-IN-PUBLICATION DATA

Marcovitz, Hal.
  Infectious mononucleosis / by Hal Marcovitz.
    p. cm. — (Diseases and disorders)
  Includes bibliographical references and index.
  ISBN 978-1-59018-938-2 (hardcover)
  1. Mononucleosis—Juvenile literature. I. Title.
  RC147.G6M37 2008
  616.9'1122—dc22

2008018287

Lucent Books
27500 Drake Rd.
Farmington Hills, MI 48331

ISBN-13: 978-1-59018-938-2
ISBN-10: 1-59018-938-8

Printed in the United States of America
1 2 3 4 5 6 7 12 11 10 09 08

Table of Contents

"The Most Difficult Puzzles Ever Devised"

Charles Best, one of the pioneers in the search for a cure for diabetes, once explained what it is about medical research that intrigued him so. "It's not just the gratification of knowing one is helping people," he confided, "although that probably is a more heroic and selfless motivation. Those feelings may enter in, but truly, what I find best is the feeling of going toe to toe with nature, of trying to solve the most difficult puzzles ever devised. The answers are there somewhere, those keys that will solve the puzzle and make the patient well. But how will those keys be found?"

Since the dawn of civilization, nothing has so puzzled people—and often frightened them, as well—as the onset of illness in a body or mind that had seemed healthy before. A seizure, the inability of a heart to pump, the sudden deterioration of muscle tone in a small child—being unable to reverse such conditions or even to understand why they occur was unspeakably frustrating to healers. Even before there were names for such conditions, even before they were understood at all, each was a reminder of how complex the human body was, and how vulnerable.

While our grappling with understanding diseases has been frustrating at times, it has also provided some of humankind's most heroic accomplishments. Alexander Fleming's accidental discovery in 1928 of a mold that could be turned into penicillin has resulted in the saving of untold millions of lives. The isolation of the enzyme insulin has reversed what was once a death sentence for anyone with diabetes. There have been great strides in combating conditions for which there is not yet a cure, too. Medicines can help AIDS patients live longer, diagnostic tools such as mammography and ultrasounds can help doctors find tumors while they are treatable, and laser surgery techniques have made the most intricate, minute operations routine.

This "toe-to-toe" competition with diseases and disorders is even more remarkable when seen in a historical continuum. An astonishing amount of progress has been made in a very short time. Just two hundred years ago, the existence of germs as a cause of some diseases was unknown. In fact, it was less than 150 years ago that a British surgeon named Joseph Lister had difficulty persuading his fellow doctors that washing their hands before delivering a baby might increase the chances of a healthy delivery (especially if they had just attended to a diseased patient)!

Each book in Lucent's Diseases and Disorders series explores a disease or disorder and the knowledge that has been accumulated (or discarded) by doctors through the years. Each book also examines the tools used for pinpointing a diagnosis, as well as the various means that are used to treat or cure a disease. Finally, new ideas are presented—techniques or medicines that may be on the horizon.

Frustration and disappointment are still part of medicine, for not every disease or condition can be cured or prevented. But the limitations of knowledge are being pushed outward constantly; the "most difficult puzzles ever devised" are finding challengers every day.

The Kissing Disease

Infectious mononucleosis is a disease that makes people very ill for a few days or weeks, then usually goes away. Patients who suffer from the disease, known familiarly as mono, may experience a number of symptoms: fever, fatigue, aches, sore throat, and other flulike ailments. After spending some time in bed, most patients get better and are back on their feet with no long-term consequences; some mono sufferers, however, may continue to feel run-down for months. In some cases, mono can lead to other illnesses that can last a lifetime. In rare cases, mono can be fatal.

Mono is spread by close contact with the saliva or mucus from another person. As such, mono has long been known as "the kissing disease," although kissing is only one way in which the disease is transmitted. Most people who contract mono are teenagers and young adults under the age of thirty. About one in every five hundred people in that age group is likely to contract mono. Although doctors may prescribe medications to ease some of the symptoms, there is no drug that clears up the infection, nor is there a vaccine that can prevent someone from contracting the illness. As British physician and medical columnist Thomas Stuttaford explains, "Infectious mononucleosis is usually a self-limiting disease. There is no treatment, but in most cases patients have recovered within a couple of weeks. In many patients, particularly children, the infection is so mild that it passes virtually unnoticed, or is confused with the flu."[1]

"Careless at Camp"

Mono has a way of stopping young people in their tracks, making them miss several days or weeks of school as well as participation in social events and athletic competitions. In addition, mono can mean days or weeks of loneliness. Few people understand that the disease is not easily spread. Even so, friends generally do not stop by to visit someone who is home sick with mono. Judith Levine Willis, editor of *FDA Consumer*, a publication of the U.S. Food and Drug Administration, writes, "Missed parties. Postponed exams. Sitting out a season of team sports. And loneliness. These are a few of the ways that scourge of high school and college students known as 'mono' can affect your life."[2]

Mono seems to hit high school and college sports teams the hardest. Each season it seems as though someone on a

Young adults are the most vulnerable to mononucleosis, often called "the kissing disease." In fact, kissing is only one way the disease is transmitted.

sports team has mono. Usually, the disease strikes one or two players, but occasionally more widespread outbreaks occur. In the fall of 2007 Diane Geist, the girls' volleyball coach at Knoch High School near Pittsburgh, Pennsylvania, was shocked when several players on the team came down with mono. "We have five girls who have been diagnosed with mono, and one who is showing signs," said Geist. "This is my twenty-second year [as coach] and I've never had anything like this before."[3]

The infected girls were among nineteen team members who attended a summer volleyball camp shortly before school started. "My guess is that they drank from the same water bottle or glass," said Geist. "We always take precautions during the season to make sure this doesn't happen. Each girl has her own water bottle to drink from during a match. They must have been careless at camp."[4]

A Compromised Immune System

Fortunately, Knoch High School was able to find a replacement players and the team stayed competitive for the season. Other teams have been devastated, though, when a key player, such as a quarterback or other star, has been forced to miss a large part of the season as he or she recovers from mono. In 2006 University of Arizona center Kirk Walters missed all but two games in his team's basketball season as he recovered from mono. A year later he still felt slowed by the disease. In 2007 fifteen-year-old Czech tennis star Nicole Vaidisova had to drop out of several tournaments as she regained her strength from a bout with mono.

And during the summer of 2007, the new Oakland Raiders head coach Lane Kiffin had to be hospitalized with an ailment that was diagnosed as mononucleosis. Kiffin started feeling ill in the team's locker room shortly after an exhibition game. Age thirty-two at the time, Kiffin was the youngest head coach in the National Football League (NFL) and clearly not that much older than the age group afflicted most by mono. Moreover, the long work hours and stressful life of an NFL head coach likely had a lot to do with breaking down Kiffin's immune system, making him a prime candidate for mono.

After taking a few days to recover, Kiffin was back on the Raiders practice field, although under a doctor's orders to take it easy. "The limitations are that I'm not supposed to do

The young women on these girls' basketball teams may lead high-pressure lives. Long hours of practice and competition may stress the body's immune system.

anything but walk out here," Kiffin said as he returned to practice. "I'm not supposed to exert energy and yell. I guess a lot of head coaches coach that way anyway, so I'm going to get to see what it's like."[5]

The experiences of Walters, Vaidosova, and Kiffin show that even highly skilled college and professional athletes and sports figures can fall victim to infectious mononucleosis. They find themselves suffering through the same aches and pains, fevers, and run-down feelings that ground thousands of young Americans each year.

CHAPTER ONE

What Is Infectious Mononucleosis?

Infectious mononucleosis was first diagnosed in 1889 by Emil Pfeiffer, a German doctor who called the disease "glandular fever" because he noticed swollen lymph nodes, or glands, in his patients. He noted the symptoms present in most of his patients: high fever for a few days or weeks, sore throat, inflammation of the liver and spleen, abdominal pain, cough, and runny nose, among others. Pfeiffer also noted that young children seemed to suffer less than adolescents and adults, but everyone seemed to get better eventually.

Within a short time, physicians in other countries confirmed Pfeiffer's analysis, and treating glandular fever became a routine part of their practices. For the most part, though, there was not much that doctors could do for glandular fever patients, other than making them comfortable and advising them to stay in bed. Indeed, the symptoms seemed to go away by themselves.

Over the next few decades, doctors learned a great deal more about glandular fever. Eventually, they determined the disease is caused by viruses. Also, through the development of a blood test, doctors were able to determine that the disease could be identified by a concentration of the white blood cells known as monocytes that the patient's body summons to fight off the infection. Monocytes are among the body's mononuclear cells, meaning they each

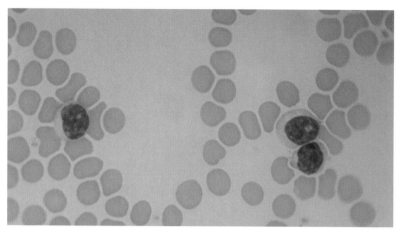

The Epstein-Barr virus is responsible for infectious mononucleosis. Here a microscopic view shows the disease's large, purple mononuclear cells.

have one nucleus. Therefore, the disease became known as infectious mononucleosis.

Identifying the Viruses

The ailment was given its nickname as the kissing disease in 1946 by Robert J. Hoagland, a physician at the U.S. Military Academy in West Point, New York, who noticed the high incidence of mono among cadets who had recently returned from leave. After questioning the cadets, Hoagland concluded that his patients contracted mono after kissing their girlfriends.

Patients who contract mono are often shocked by the diagnosis—particularly teenagers who are not in romantic relationships. They may ask, "How can I get the kissing disease when I have not kissed anyone in weeks?" The answer is that mono typically takes from thirty to fifty days to manifest itself in symptoms. This means that if a teenage girl breaks up with her boyfriend in October, she may not start feeling ill until November or December. And just because the patient has not been in a romantic relationship in months does not mean he or she is safe from mono.

Somebody who shares a drinking glass, a straw, or eating utensils with a mono carrier can contract the disease. The disease can also be contracted by somebody who simply finds himself or herself in the same room with a carrier who has coughed or sneezed. The tiny droplets of mucus or saliva that float through a room after a mono carrier sneezes or coughs can easily be inhaled by others. "Many viruses are transmitted by droplet infection, the euphemistic phrase used by doctors to describe the spread of disease by small drops of spittle and nasal discharge, which, laden with a potpourri of organisms, are scattered with every cough and sneeze," says physician and columnist Thomas Stuttaford. "Kissing delivers an even larger dose."[6]

There are two viruses that spread mono: the Epstein-Barr virus (EBV), which is responsible for about 85 percent of all mono cases, and cytomegalovirus (CMV), which spreads the rest. Viruses are organisms that are transmitted from one living thing to another. EBV and CMV are members of the herpes family of viruses. Herpes viruses can also manifest themselves in cold sores, genital herpes, chicken pox, and other illnesses.

EBV is named for the two British researchers, Michael Epstein and Yvonne Barr, who identified the virus in 1964. CMV

The Epstein-Barr virus, shown here highly magnified (larger picture), is responsible for most cases of mono. In the inset is the less common cytomegalovirus.

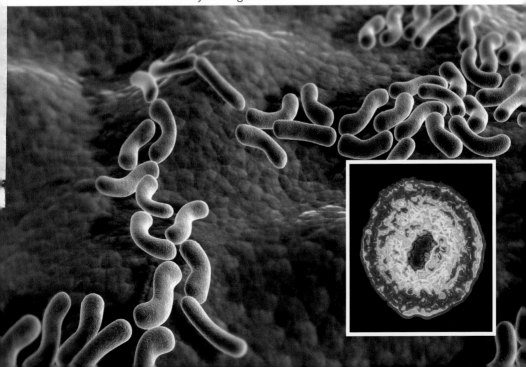

was discovered in the 1950s. It is believed that EBV and CMV have become so widespread in the United States and in other industrialized nations that as many as 95 percent of people in those countries will have been exposed to them by the time they reach the age of forty.

In most cases, people who contract EBV and CMV show no symptoms. This is particularly true of young children, half of whom contract EBV before the age of five. With EBV and CMV already in their bodies, they have built up natural immunities against the viruses; it is not likely that they will ever suffer symptoms.

What mono patients may find puzzling is how they managed to contract mono from someone who did not appear to be ill. Yet carriers do not have to show mono symptoms to be contagious. In fact, the active forms of EBV and CMV remain in their throats for long periods after they recover from their own mono symptoms, meaning that weeks or months after they shake off mono, their coughs or kisses can still infect others.

Even so, mono is not regarded as highly contagious. Large-scale outbreaks are rare. That is because of the natural immunity most people have built up against mononucleosis. Therefore, it is unlikely that friends and family members who visit a recuperating mono patient will develop symptoms themselves.

Common Symptoms

Although anyone can contract mono, teenagers and young adults who have not yet been exposed to EBV or CMV are the most susceptible. According to the U.S. Centers for Disease Control and Prevention, the federal agency that tracks trends in public health, a teenager or young adult who has not previously been exposed to EBV has a 35 to 50 percent chance of coming down with mono if he or she comes into contact with the viruses, either through a kiss or similar form of exposure.

The first sign that someone is ill with mono shows up in the lymph nodes—the glands identified by Pfeiffer. Lymph nodes are the body's natural filters that fight infection and trap viruses and bacteria. They are located in the armpits, neck, groin, and

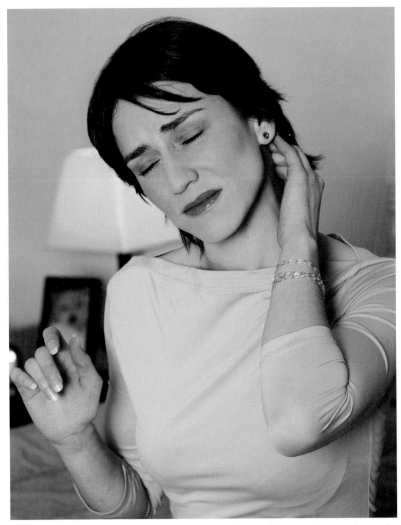

A woman massages a painful lymph node on her neck. Lymph node inflammation is an early sign of mono infection.

elbows. When the body fights off an infection, the lymph nodes summon white blood cells, which is why they become inflamed. This is particularly true when the body fights off EBV.

Most mono patients who notice the swollen areas in their necks or under their arms do not immediately run to their doctors. In most cases, the swollen glands are little more than a mild inconvenience—parts of the body that, for some reason, seem to feel a bit tender. "[Swollen lymph nodes], detected by the patients themselves, is rarely a presenting symptom of infectious mononucleosis, but most patients are aware of this abnormality at some time during the illness,"[7] says S.C. Finch, a doctor of internal medicine at Yale University Medical School in New Haven, Connecticut.

Soon, though, mono patients will feel ill in many other ways. Symptoms such as coughing, chills, and a runny nose are common and are responsible for many mono patients wrongly diagnosing themselves with the flu.

Next, many mono patients experience very sore throats, along with white patches on the backs of their throats as well as swollen tonsils, which are lymph glands located in the throat. "My tonsils got so swollen they were touching each other in back,"[8] says Heidi Palombo, a Virginia student who came down with mono in college. Palombo says her throat became so swollen that she had difficulty swallowing and that the only relief she could find was by drinking ice water. Typically, a sore throat will develop a few days after the onset of the disease, will grow increasingly painful for about a week, and then will subside. As Finch explains, "In some patients the sore throat is hardly noticed, in the majority it is mild, but in a few it is so severe that swallowing even a few sips of water is extremely painful."[9]

Headaches are common among mono patients. Most mono patients report mild headaches, but occasionally they can become quite painful. Some mono patients say they have difficulty seeing because their eyelids become very puffy. Mono patients have also reported that their eyes become very sensitive to light. As such, they prefer to have the blinds drawn in their bedrooms. Some mono patients have also complained about toothaches.

Nausea and vomiting are common symptoms. Mono patients may have to endure stomach ailments for several days, making it difficult for them to eat or keep food in their stomachs. The extreme sore throats suffered by mono patients also make them want to turn down food.

Mono patients tend to run very high fevers; a temperature as high as 103 degrees Fahrenheit (39.5°C) is not unusual.

According to Finch, "A physical finding of considerable significance in virtually all patients with infectious mononucleosis is the presence of fever with daily peak temperatures usually between 100 and 103 degrees Fahrenheit."[10] Indeed, it is the high fever—as well as the very sore throat—that prompts most mono patients to see their doctors.

Enlarged Livers and Spleens

There are other symptoms that may not be apparent to a patient but a doctor can usually detect them. For example, most mono patients have slow heart rates—a condition known as bradycardia—that the doctor can determine by timing the patient's pulse, usually by using a stethoscope. Typically, the pulse rate for mono patients will slow to fewer than sixty beats per minute. Also, fewer than 6 percent of mono patients develop a mild skin rash that may disappear a few days after the onset of the other symptoms. Patients tend not to notice the rash—perhaps because they are so ill in other ways—but the trained eye of a doctor may be able to find it.

Mono may attack and inflame the liver, one of the body's vital organs. A doctor may be able to detect an inflamed liver by examining a patient's upper right abdomen, where the liver is located. An inflamed liver is known as hepatitis, a potentially serious condition that could lead to long-term illness and even death if the swelling is not brought under control. Such complications are rare in mono patients; the liver usually returns to normal size as the other symptoms recede. Still, a common symptom of hepatitis is jaundice, a yellowing of the skin and eyes caused by the failure of the liver to expel bile, a fluid that assists in digestion. About 10 percent of mono patients will develop temporary jaundice.

Another organ attacked by mono is the spleen, which is located near the liver. The spleen's function is to dispose of old blood cells. Mono often causes the spleen to become enlarged. Patients usually have no way of telling that their spleens are enlarged, but a doctor can feel very subtle changes in the organ, indicating that the spleen is inflamed. Unlike the other

Infectious Mononucleosis in Older Adults

Infectious mononucleosis is regarded as a disease that mostly strikes teenagers and young adults, but older people are not immune. Studies have found that between 3 and 10 percent of adults over the age of sixty have never been exposed to the Epstein-Barr virus and are, therefore, prime candidates to contract mono.

Still, mono cases among older adults are considered rare. About one in five hundred people under the age of thirty are likely to contract mono. In people over the age of thirty-four, the incidence of mono drops to one or two per fifty thousand.

Older mono patients tend to suffer more than younger patients. In particular, their livers become inflamed, and they usually suffer from jaundice, symptoms that are less common in younger patients. Also, studies show that older mono patients tend to run higher fevers than younger patients and that their fevers may last longer. One recent study reported that older mono patients typically endure high fevers for an average of thirteen days; in younger patients, the high fevers usually abate after about seven days. As Barbara Homeier, a Delaware pediatrician, relates, "The older you get, the harder it seems to hit."

Quoted in Kirsten Weir, "Oh, No! Mono," *Current Health 2*, September 2005, p. 12.

symptoms, the spleen often does not return to normal after a few days or weeks. Instead, the spleen may remain enlarged for several weeks after the mono seems to have passed. That is why people who have recently recovered from mono are advised to do no strenuous activity for several weeks following the illness. Doctors fear that they may bruise or even rupture their spleens, which could cause internal bleeding.

Extreme Fatigue

Clearly, the most common symptom of mono is the extreme fatigue that afflicts patients. During the peak of their illnesses, most mono patients lack the energy to get out of bed. Many simply want to sleep. Even after spending several hours each day and night asleep, they still feel fatigued. In many cases, for weeks after they have recovered from their runny noses, sore throats, high fevers, and swollen lymph glands, mono patients find themselves enduring several periods in which they seem to lack energy. As Finch explains, "Full activity in most patients is commonly resumed four to five weeks from the onset of the illness, but in others it may be delayed for several weeks."[11] One mono patient, fifteen-year-old Audrey Warnez of Ortonville, Michigan, recalls the tremendous effort it took just to get out of bed. "I was so tired, I would walk up the stairs and feel like I needed to take a nap,"[12] she says.

Athletes find the fatigue particularly frustrating. Even though they may otherwise feel fine, athletes find themselves lacking the energy they have always been able to summon to compete on a high level. Indeed, mono can be devastating to a high school or college athletic career. A football player contracting mono in his senior year of high school may lose his last chance to play competitively. College athletes who compete on very high levels may be thrown off training regimens that may take months to return to normal. In the meantime, they may lose a year or more of their eligibility to compete in interscholastic sports.

That is what happened to Erin Bedell, a cross-country and track star at Baylor University in Texas. Bedell was sidelined by fatigue for a year after she recovered from her other mono symptoms. In the meantime, Bedell was forced to sit out the school's 2006 cross-country season. In the spring of 2007, Bedell thought she felt well enough to compete on the Baylor track team, but she was soon forced to sit out that season as well. By the fall of 2007, she was just starting to compete at the level she had attained before the illness. "With (mono), you can't recuperate as fast," she says. "In the spring, I had a mini-relapse after indoor (track) season, because I tried to come back too fast. . . . It's been really hard, because I didn't do workouts for my event for a whole year. So the season has been really tough and definitely a challenge for me."[13]

Even if they do quickly regain their strength, athletes are usually advised to sit on the bench for three weeks or more after they have recovered from mono in case their spleens are still enlarged. As Delaware pediatrician Barbara Homeier states, "If you're cheerleading or playing football and you get hit, your spleen could rupture. If your spleen ruptures, you can bleed to death very quickly."[14]

Chronic Mononucleosis

When mono patients finally recover, they may feel a tremendous elation—as though they have been released from prison after long sentences. They are able to return to their schools or

An athlete suffering the debilitating fatigue of a mono infection sits on the bench during a game.

teams or attend social events where they can see their friends, probably for the first time in several weeks. Audrey Warnez contracted mono in June—a month when school winds down and summer activities begin. When Warnez started feeling better, she was happy to get out of the house so she could begin enjoying her summer vacation. "June is my favorite month, and I had to stay inside and not go anywhere for the entire time," Warnez said. "I was so mad, I was livid!"[15]

In some cases, that elation may be short-lived. Mono patients can occasionally suffer a relapse. They find themselves afflicted with what is known as recurrent or chronic mononucleosis. For years, doctors did not believe it was possible. They were convinced that once the symptoms subsided, mono patients had developed a natural immunity and their symptoms would not be repeated. But in recent years, physicians have found it hard to deny the evidence. They now believe that some mono patients may develop new symptoms months or even years after they recover from their initial experiences.

As a young woman Ann Japenga of Palm Springs, California, suffered through a bout of mono. Fifteen years later she suffered a relapse. In describing the onset of symptoms, she says:

> My virus debuted innocently enough. I was driving to a conference from my home in Southern California and, halfway there, I didn't feel well enough to go on. So I turned the car around and headed home. Over the following weeks I felt flu-ish and lead-limbed, but assumed it was due to allergies or a passing bug.
>
> But it became apparent it was something more. I had to quit daily swims because I was shaking after ten minutes in the water. . . . Eventually, I was too sick to talk on the phone for more than a few minutes.
>
> My lymph nodes puffed up and my liver swelled so much it hurt to sit upright. I lost eighteen pounds and was tormented by viral shakes, as if an outboard motor was

Kissing Under the Mistletoe

The quaint Christmastime custom of kissing under the mistletoe may help spread infectious mononucleosis. Under the tradition, a twig of mistletoe—an evergreen plant that sprouts berries—is tacked overhead. When couples kiss under the mistletoe, they remove a berry. When all the berries have been plucked, the mistletoe is said to no longer possess the power to promote love. Therefore, latecomers who find themselves under the mistletoe with no berries to pluck are out of luck—they will not fall in love.

According to Thomas Stuttaford, a British physician and medical columnist, the truly lucky people are the ones who find themselves under the mistletoe with no berries to pluck. "They may have been more fortunate than they supposed and missed out on more than the transitory pleasure of a kiss," he says. "From a medical point of view, late December could not be a worse time of year to scatter kisses around previously casual friends."

Indeed, physicians believe wintertime is a prime breeding time for mono because most people spend a lot of time indoors and in close quarters, making it more likely that they will come into contact with carriers of the Epstein-Barr virus.

Thomas Stuttaford, "It Started with a Kiss," *Times of London,* December 20, 2001.

rattling my bones. A blood test showed high levels of antibodies to the Epstein-Barr virus. . . .

EBV is common and, usually, benign. By adulthood, most of us have been exposed to it and suffer little for the encounter, except perhaps a teenage round of mono. But in susceptible hosts the virus hits hard and relentlessly. It can go underground and recur years later.

That's what happened to me. I'd had a long bout of mono fifteen years earlier, and this time around the virus was ten times worse. Months went by and I was still sick.[16]

Japenga eventually recovered from her second bout of mono, but for many other patients some of the effects from the disease can last indefinitely. Indeed, some mono patients go on to suffer through episodes of fatigue for years after they recover from their initial experiences with mono. This malady is known as chronic fatigue syndrome.

Bouncing Back

Although mono can often send its patients to bed for weeks, for most people the illness is temporary. According to Finch, "Patients with uncomplicated infectious mononucleosis usually require little more than rest in bed during the acute phase of the illness. Isolation is unnecessary."[17] Indeed, Judith Levine Willis, the *FDA Consumer* editor who suffered through a bout of mono herself at the age of sixteen, recalls that she was able to handle the aches and pains, but what really concerned her was delaying her finals and her college applications, and whether her boyfriend would call again. "Getting through mono may be both challenging and depressing—and seem to take forever," she says. "But if you rest when your body tells you to, you can lessen your chances of complications and get back your life."[18]

Mono can be unpleasant. The headaches, flulike symptoms, nausea, sore throats, and fatigue can wear anybody down. There is no question, though, that most mono patients find that after a very temporary period of illness, they can eventually bounce back.

CHAPTER TWO

Can Mononucleosis Spark Other Diseases?

In most patients, infectious mononucleosis will clear up with no long-term complications. In some cases, however, patients who have suffered through bouts of mono may face other, much more severe illnesses. In recent years, medical researchers have found high incidences of multiple sclerosis, heart attack, Guillain-Barré syndrome, and some cancers among former patients of the viruses that cause mono.

At this point, medical researchers do not believe that mono causes those other illnesses. Instead, researchers have concluded that some patients may have compromised immune systems due to their battles against the Epstein-Barr virus (EBV) and cytomegalovirus (CMV). With their immune systems weakened by the two viruses, other diseases may be able to do more damage in the patients' bodies. Still, researchers are also studying whether EBV or CMV may actually trigger the other illnesses.

Meanwhile, medical researchers are only beginning to understand the causes and complications associated with chronic fatigue syndrome (CFS). Once known as the "yuppie flu" because it seemed mostly to afflict young professionals, or "yuppies," CFS was long questioned by doctors who could find no cause. Now it has been determined that some CFS patients have a history of mononucleosis, and EBV is seen as the culprit that could be causing millions of Americans to suffer through long-term and relentless bouts of fatigue and other symptoms.

As for most of the teenagers and young adults who are suffering through mononucleosis, they should take comfort in knowing that in a few days or weeks they will start feeling better. Still, doctors are likely to be closely monitoring their conditions because, in some cases, mono can cause serious consequences. For example, in patients with extremely sore throats, doctors worry that their throats may close completely, cutting off the air supply to their lungs. Another worry for doctors is that fluid will accumulate in the lungs of patients. In rare cases, such complications from mono have caused death.

Common Complications

Although mono is a common illness suffered by many people, the large majority of whom recover after a brief period of time, doctors still monitor the symptoms closely. Complications can occur in any disease, including mono. Indeed, between 3 and 5 percent

The open mouth of a mono patient shows the red, swollen lymph glands and sore throat typical of the disease.

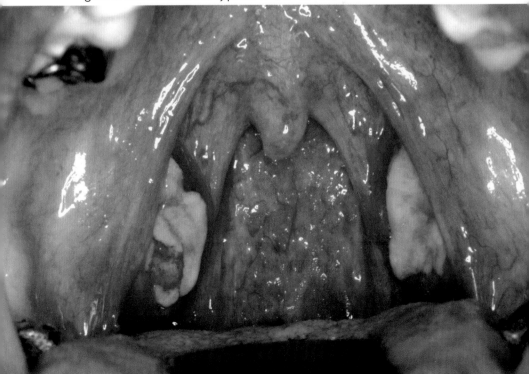

of mono patients suffer from an accumulation of fluid in their lungs, which is also known as Epstein-Barr virus pneumonia. In most cases, the condition clears up on its own, but physicians may prescribe drugs to reduce the inflammation in the lungs.

In fewer than 1 percent of mono patients, the infection spreads to the brain, causing meningitis or encephalitis. Meningitis is an inflammation of the meninges—the thin layers of tissue that surround and protect the brain and spinal cord. When the meninges become inflamed, the patient may experience a series of debilitating symptoms, including fever, nausea, vomiting, headaches, dizziness, stiff necks, and other joint pain. Encephalitis is an inflammation of the brain; its symptoms are similar to those of meningitis. If mono develops into meningitis or encephalitis, physicians may order the patient hospitalized for observation; in most cases, however, these complications tend to clear up on their own. Yale University physician S.C. Finch states, "Most of these conditions are transient and annoying, but pose no real problem in patient management."[19]

Of much more concern to doctors, though, is the sore throat that accompanies virtually all mono cases. If it appears as though the throat is swelling to the point where it could block air flow to the lungs, the physician will likely prescribe drugs to reduce the inflammation.

Suffocation due to closure of the throat is one of the ways in which mono patients can succumb to the disease. Mono patients can also die from internal bleeding due to the rupture of their spleens. For the most part, though, death is an extremely rare outcome of mononucleosis; according to Finch, the death rate among mono patients is probably less than a tenth of 1 percent. Nevertheless, there are fatal cases of mono on record. In fact, a 2001 study by a team of Japanese physicians listed ten "life-threatening complications"[20] from infections associated with the Epstein-Barr virus, including mono. Among those complications listed in the study were infections of the liver, lungs, heart, blood, and central nervous system, all of which can develop from cases of mono.

Because death is such a rare outcome of mono, when it strikes it can be a devastating consequence of the disease because it is so unexpected. Years after the death of her sister Pam, Paula Behr still feels shocked by her loss. Pam and Paula were twins. At the age of seventeen, the two girls each contracted mono. Paula recovered, but Pam's immune system shut down; after eleven days in a Duluth, Minnesota, hospital, Pam died. "I swear I felt the soul leave her body,"[21] Paula Behr says.

Parents of young children who contract mono must also be wary. Although children seem to suffer fewer symptoms, parents must refrain from giving them aspirin. Research has shown that young children who consume aspirin to fight off viral infections, such as mono or chicken pox, risk contracting Reye's syndrome, a potentially fatal disease that attacks the brain and liver. Evidently, the ingredients in aspirin may spark the onset of the syndrome in a young patient whose immunity has already been weakened by mono or a similar infection.

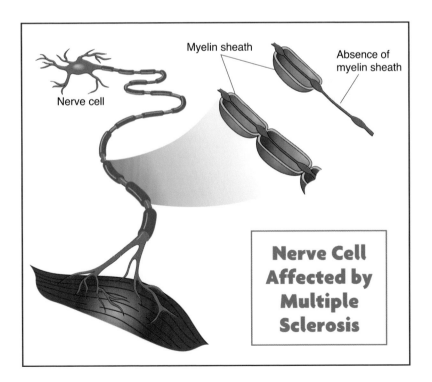

Myelin sheath

Absence of myelin sheath

Nerve cell

Nerve Cell Affected by Multiple Sclerosis

Lewis Carroll and the Epstein-Barr Virus

Lewis Carroll, the author of *Alice's Adventures in Wonderland*, may have suffered from a rare ailment associated with the Epstein-Barr virus: a mental condition in which one's perception of reality is widely altered. In his book, Carroll—whose real name was Charles Lutwidge Dodgson—writes about Alice chasing the white rabbit down a very long rabbit hole, at the bottom of which she finds a tiny door. To fit through the door, Alice drinks a potion that enables her to shrink; then, after walking through the door, she eats a piece of cake that makes her grow into a giant.

"It is believed Dodgson may have been describing his own symptoms," says Australian physician and medical columnist Adam Taor. "This curious syndrome is occasionally associated with Epstein-Barr virus." The ailment is known as Alice in Wonderland syndrome. Although sufferers of the syndrome may be startled by the symptoms, they do not last long.

According to Taor, "While the symptoms may be terrifying, it's believed when associated with Epstein-Barr virus, they resolve without serious complications. Fortunately, they are very rare."

Adam Taor, "A Bug's Life," *Australian*, June 18, 2005.

Charles Lutwidge Dodgson, whose pen name was Lewis Carroll, may have incorporated some of his own symptoms in his Alice books.

Links to Other Diseases

While physicians closely monitor mono symptoms to ensure they do not become life-threatening, more and more research is surfacing that indicates mono may be at the root of a number of other illnesses. For example, it is believed that about a quarter of Guillain-Barré syndrome patients have a history of illnesses sparked by EBV or CMV, including mono. Guillain-Barré syndrome can cause nerve damage, paralysis, and respiratory distress in patients. Usually, patients make a full recovery; however, if left untreated, the syndrome can cause respiratory failure.

Guillain-Barré syndrome is not believed to be contagious. Still, there are occasions when the syndrome seems to occur in waves. In the spring of 1996 eight residents of Bergen County, New Jersey, contracted Guillain-Barré. One young girl who contracted the disease, six-year-old Valerie Pickett, had just recovered from a bout of mono when she developed Guillain-Barré symptoms. After sledding with friends, Valerie complained to her mother of a tingling feeling in her fingers and toes. A day later, she could not stand up. "She had jelly legs,"[22] says her mother, Julie Pickett. The young girl was hospitalized and a short time later started recovering from her paralysis.

Another disease that is being studied for links to mono is multiple sclerosis (MS). The disease attacks a fatty layer, known as myelin, that insulates and protects nerves in the brain and spine, which make up the central nervous system. The nerves carry commands from the brain to the rest of the body through a series of electrical impulses. MS disrupts those signals, meaning that the body does not receive clear commands from the brain. People who contract MS often experience fatigue, nerve damage, partial paralysis, numbness, loss of coordination, defects to their vision, and damage to their brains that makes it difficult for them to communicate and think clearly.

MS is an autoimmune disease, meaning that it is caused when the body attacks its own immune system. At Harvard University in Cambridge, Massachusetts, medical researchers have found evidence suggesting that people who have summoned a large number of white blood cells to fight illnesses sparked by EBV, including mono, are more prone than others to develop MS. Therefore, it is believed that MS may strike a body that has been weakened by EBV. "It is almost as if the virus sets the stage for the development of multiple sclerosis,"[23] says Patricia K. Coyle, acting chairwoman of the neurology department at Stony Brook University Hospital in New York.

Meanwhile, other studies have found the viruses that cause mononucleosis may be responsible for weakening the heart and leading to such diseases as cardiomyopathy, which is a deterioration of the heart muscle, and atherosclerosis, a narrowing of the arteries that lead to the heart. A 2002 study published in *Circulation: Journal of the American Heart Association* found that 70 percent of patients who have experienced heart disease have high levels of CMV in their bodies. The researchers suggested that CMV may place stress on the heart. "This increased stress on the heart triggers pathways that lead to heart failure,"[24] says Kenneth Chien, lead author of the study and director of molecular medicine at the University of California at San Diego.

A separate study, also conducted in 2002 at the University of Mainz in Germany, found that people who suffer from multiple infectious diseases are likely to suffer heart disease more so than others. According to the study, one of the infectious diseases that contribute to weak hearts is EBV. The study found that the death rate among people who experience four or five infectious diseases is five times higher than people who experience just one of the viral infections.

EBV and Cancer

One disease that has been definitely linked to EBV is a form of cancer known as Burkitt's lymphoma. It is a rare but particularly horrific disease, first discovered in Africa in 1958 by a Ugandan doctor, Denis Burkitt. Burkitt's lymphoma attacks the immune system, causing swelling to the lymph nodes in the neck, groin, and under the arms. Burkitt's lymphoma afflicts the abdomen, head, and neck of the patient, where tumors often grow at tremendously fast rates. The disease spreads quickly to other parts of the body, usually resulting in the death of the patient.

EBV was found to be the cause of Burkitt's lymphoma in 1964. In fact, Michael Epstein and Yvonne Barr were studying

An African child ravaged by Burkitt's lymphoma presents the classic symptoms of the disease.

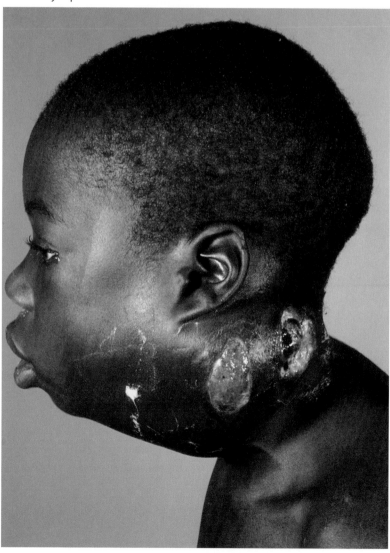

Burkitt's lymphoma when they discovered the virus that would bear their names. EBV is one of the few viruses known to medical science that can take healthy cells and make them cancerous.

Another cancer linked to EBV is nasopharyngeal cancer (NPC), which afflicts an area of the body located at the back of the nose near the skull, but it can also spread to the throat and other places. Is it likely that people who experience bouts of mononucleosis will go on to develop Burkitt's lymphoma or NPC. If they live in the United States or other industrialized countries, they probably have little to fear. Burkitt's lymphoma is found mostly in central Africa and New Guinea, places where tropical conditions are common. The fact that Burkitt's lymphoma is virtually unheard of outside of tropical climates has prompted medical researchers to speculate that something else must act in concert with EBV in order for the disease to progress to Burkitt's lymphoma. Some researchers have suggested that Burkitt's lymphoma may be caused by a combination of EBV and malaria, a disease spread by mosquitoes in some tropical climates. According to William Dameshek, a professor of medicine at Tufts University in Medford, Massachusetts, "EB virus, which has been implicated in both Burkitt's lymphoma and infectious mononucleosis, may only have a 'passenger' relationship to these two diseases or it may be the direct cause of both, or it may, by its ubiquity, have the capability of causing a reaction . . . when opportunity presents."[25]

As for NPC, former mononucleosis patients in industrialized countries would appear to have little to fear from that disease as well. The disease strikes mostly in southern China as well as in parts of Africa, the Middle East, and Greenland. Diet is believed to be a contributing factor; many patients are found to have vitamin C deficiencies in their bodies, which may compromise their immune systems and make them more susceptible to EBV complications.

Burkitt's lymphoma and NPC are found mostly in Africa and other parts of the developing world. In recent years, however,

David Vetter, the Bubble Boy

One of the saddest stories associated with the Epstein-Barr virus involves a young boy named David Vetter, who was born in 1971 with a rare condition known as severe combined immunodeficiency (SCID). The condition meant that David's body had no immunity against disease and that exposure to any germ could be fatal. Shortly after his birth, David was placed inside a germfree plastic bubble, where he would remain until a cure could be found for SCID.

After spending twelve years in the bubble, physicians suggested that David's body could develop immunity if he received a bone marrow transplant from his sister, Katherine. Bone marrow is the soft tissue on the inside of the bones. It is an important component of the body because new blood cells are created in bone marrow.

In late 1983 Katherine's bone marrow was injected into her brother's body. A short time later David grew ill and developed cancer of the lymph glands. He died in February 1984. After his death it was determined that Katherine's bone marrow contained the Epstein-Barr virus, which sparked the cancer in David's body.

David Vetter plays in his specially constructed germfree plastic environment.

researchers have explored the relationship between EBV and cancers that are common in the United States and other industrialized nations, particularly Hodgkin's disease, which is a cancer of the lymph glands. The disease—which was named for its discoverer, British physician Thomas Hodgkin—causes the lymph nodes to grow abnormally and breaks down the body's ability to fight infection. In the United States each year, there are about eight thousand cases of Hodgkin's disease, including about thirteen hundred that are fatal. Studies have shown that people who have contracted EBV-related illnesses, including mono, are four times more likely than others to contract Hodgkin's disease.

Chronic Fatigue Syndrome

Some of the symptoms of Hodgkin's disease are similar to those common in mono cases—swollen lymph glands, relentless fatigue, loss of appetite, and fever, among others. Hodgkin's disease can be detected through a number of accurate tests, including an examination of tissue in the lymph nodes as well as tests of the blood. If treated successfully through chemotherapy and radiation, Hodgkin's disease patients can recover fully and rid their bodies of the symptoms. Indeed, diseases such as cancer can be diagnosed with a high degree of certainty and, when doctors know what they are dealing with, a treatment program can be established for the patient.

However, one disease associated with EBV has often defied the efforts of physicians to diagnose the cause of the condition. This disease is chronic fatigue syndrome. "This is a fatigue unlike a fatigue you've ever experienced," says Michelle Lapuk, a founder of the Connecticut Fatigue and Immune Dysfunction Syndrome Association. "This is, 'Can I lift the toothbrush to brush my teeth?' tired."[26]

Severe fatigue appears to be just one symptom of CFS. Other symptoms reported by patients include migraine headaches, nausea, respiratory stress, aching muscles, persistent sore throat, swollen lymph glands, difficulty concentrating, poor memory, fever, low blood pressure, indigestion, sensitivity to bright lights and loud sounds, loss of appetite, difficulty sleeping, depression, and muscle spasms. But, as the name suggests, it is the crushing fatigue that afflicts most patients. One noted sufferer is Stephen Lewis, the former Canadian ambassador to the United Nations. In 1991 he had to take virtually the whole year off from a busy diplomatic schedule to recover from CFS. "It was so bizarre, it's hard to phrase it," Lewis says. "I was simply clobbered. I was inert . . . I couldn't stand it. To be so completely immobilized was the most depressing period of my adult life."[27]

In the past, what made the disease so particularly frustrating to patients was that there did not seem to be a reason for it. Doctors would put their CFS patients through a battery of tests and find nothing wrong, a fact that prompted many doctors—and the employers of patients who were missing months of work—to wonder whether the patients were not simply lazy. Because the disease seems to frequently hit young working adults, CFS is sometimes referred to as "yuppie flu." Skeptics had a different word for it: They called it "shirker syndrome." Linda Dooley of Warwick, Rhode Island, is a typical patient. She was forced to miss two years of work while trying to convince people that she truly was sick. "I couldn't feed myself, I couldn't wash myself, I couldn't brush my hair, but no one could tell me what was wrong," she says. "No one could believe I was in pain until they saw my muscles go into spasms and start twitching."[28]

In 1984 medical research finally started finding links between CFS and EBV. Research has also indicated that many CFS sufferers are former mono patients. As more studies were performed, they turned up more cases of CFS, indicating that the disease was rather widespread and not limited to just a few malingerers. In 1987 Brigham and Women's Hospital in Boston identified EBV in five hundred CFS patients. According to Anthony L. Komaroff, the chief of general medicine at the hospital, "Every time I say to a friend that I'm studying this illness, and then describe it, they say, 'Oh, my God. My niece has it, or my next-door neighbor, or my boss.'"[29]

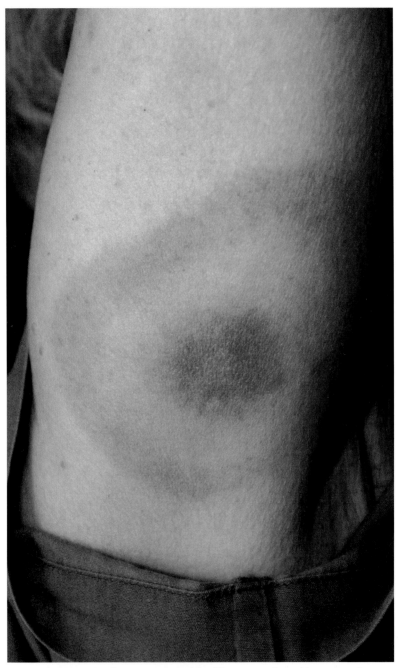

Lyme disease produces a typical bull's-eye rash at the site of a deer tick bite on a woman's arm.

A New Emphasis on Research

Still, more than two decades after the first links between CFS and EBV were established, medical research has yet to prove that EBV is the definitive cause of CFS. One of the most recent studies into the links between EBV and CFS was completed in 2006. Researchers in Australia studied twenty-nine CFS sufferers in the rural township of Dubbo and concluded that five of the patients had evidence of past EBV-related illnesses, including mono. The CFS patients suffered from various other infections. These included Q fever, which is caused by the inhalation of particles of feces and urine from animals such as dogs, cats, sheep, and cattle; and Ross River virus, which is spread by mosquitoes, mostly in Australia, and manifests itself in joint pain, fever, and rash. The Australian study indicated that although EBV may be one cause of CFS, there are likely to be other causes as well. Indeed, other recent studies have linked CFS to Lyme disease, a debilitating illness spread by ticks. Kimberly Mc-Clearly, the president of the Chronic Fatigue and Immune Dysfunction Syndrome Association, says, "It's unlikely that this big cluster of people who fit the symptoms all have the same triggers."[30]

Clearly, though, as the new revelations about CFS indicate, there is a lot about EBV as well as mono that are still not fully understood by physicians and medical researchers. However, no longer do physicians and others doubt the words of CFS sufferers. Their complaints are taken seriously, particularly by the Centers for Disease Control and Prevention (CDC), which has placed a new emphasis on investigating the disease. For example, the agency has released a study indicating that the genetic makeup of CFS patients may make them more prone to contract the disease. In other words, CFS could be a condition passed down from generation to generation.

In addition, the CDC believes better diagnostic techniques are needed to determine exactly who has the disease. In the past, the agency suggested that patients needed to exhibit at least four symptoms of CFS for no less than six months before a diagnosis of the disease could be made. Under that criterion, it was believed that about a million Americans suffer from CFS.

Now, though, the CDC is considering a new criterion for the diagnosis of CFS. The agency is reviewing a study conducted in Georgia in 2004 and 2005, in which people were diagnosed with CFS if they reported just one symptom for a duration of at least one month. Under the criteria used in the Georgia study, it was found that at least one adult in forty between the ages of eighteen and fifty-nine may suffer from CFS—a rate estimated at six to ten times higher than previously reported rates of CFS.

In fact, the CDC has conceded that it was wrong to ignore the illness. In 2007 the federal agency acknowledged that for years it had diverted millions of dollars earmarked by Congress for CFS studies into other research programs under the belief that there was no such illness. In making the acknowledgment, CDC officials announced that the agency intended to launch a $6 million campaign to make physicians and others aware of CFS symptoms. As William Reeves, the director of the CFS program at the CDC, explains, "People with CFS are as sick and as functionally impaired as someone with AIDS [or] with breast cancer."[31]

CHAPTER THREE

A Difficult Diagnosis

Infectious mononucleosis presents a wide array of symptoms—high fever, sore throat, swollen lymph glands, headache, runny nose, enlarged liver and spleen, as well as many others. As such, mono can fool doctors, who may mistake it for other illnesses that exhibit similar symptoms.

College students who show up at their campus health centers complaining of fevers and sore throats are often advised that they have the flu and should get some bed rest. Tonsillitis is another common misdiagnosis. When doctors see the inflamed tonsils at the back of the throat, they often prescribe antibiotics such as penicillin to clear up the infections. Since mono will not respond to antibiotics, this remedy will not work. Therefore, patients likely will be back in their offices a few days later. One student, John L. Gipson of Kansas City, Missouri, showed up at his doctor's office with a rash and was told he had suffered a bite from a spider. "That's what I thought because I had killed a spider in my room. I figured I'd been bitten by a spider in my sleep. A few days later . . . I had no energy, a fever and those peasized bumps on the back of my neck,"[32] he says. When Gipson returned, the doctor ordered a blood test and correctly diagnosed the patient with mono.

As in Gipson's case, when the patient returns with the same symptoms, the doctor will typically order a monospot test. In most cases, the monospot test will reveal mono, but the test is not foolproof—it is inaccurate in as many as 15 percent of cases. An inconclusive monospot test may prompt the doctor to look for other causes of the symptoms, putting the patient through a series of needless tests and perhaps prescribing drugs that will have no effect.

Much more serious are the cases in which a severe disease has been misdiagnosed as mono. Leukemia, which is a form of cancer, is often mistaken for mono. Lyme disease is another common ailment that is often misdiagnosed as mono. Lyme disease should be treated with antibiotics, but if the doctor is convinced the illness is mono, no drugs will be prescribed. This means that the unfortunate Lyme sufferer will receive no relief until the diagnosis is corrected.

The Monospot Test

The first test for mono is always a physical examination conducted by the doctor. When a patient complains of severe sore throat, high fever, and some of the other common mono symptoms, the doctor will examine the lymph glands to see if they are swollen. The doctor will also feel the abdomen, searching for subtle changes in the liver and spleen that could indicate they are enlarged. Usually, the physician can make a preliminary diagnosis of mono based on the symptoms he or she observes during the physical examination. The doctor may want confirmation, though, and will order the monospot test, which is an analysis of the patient's blood. The test will look for a concentration of monocyte blood cells, indicating that the body is fighting off EBV or CMV.

To conduct the monospot test, blood will be drawn from the patient's vein. Once the patient has developed symptoms of mono, it could take as little as a week for the body to summon monocyte cells in concentrations that will be indicated by the test. But in some patients, it can take as long as three weeks. Thus, if the test is administered before the monocyte cells are gathered in concentrations that can be counted by the test, the results will come back negative. In addition, a small number of mono patients simply do not summon enough monocyte cells to be counted. They still have mono, but for reasons doctors

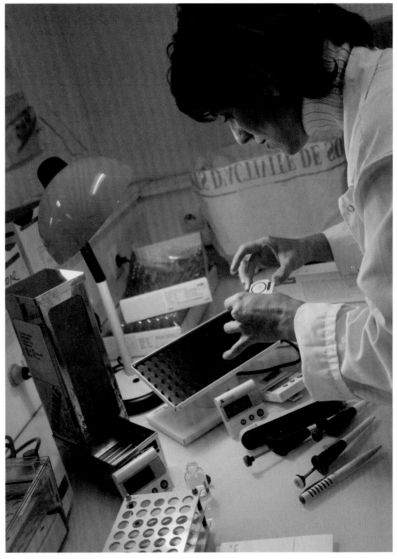

A lab technician analyzes the results of a patient's monospot test. The test looks for a concentration of monocytes.

cannot explain, their bodies summon fewer monocyte cells than most other mono patients. In their cases, the monospot test may miss the disease.

The case of Amanda Walters serves as a typical example of what could go wrong during a mono examination. Walters, a freshman at Ball State University in Muncie, Indiana, felt sick and went to her university's health center, where she was told she had strep throat. The doctor prescribed antibiotics. After two weeks, she still felt ill. Walters called home and told her mother about her symptoms. Her mother, who had contracted mono as a college freshman, urged Walters to go back to the health center. Walters followed her mother's advice, returned to the health center, and asked to be tested for mono. The staff administered the monospot test, but it came back negative. A week later, still feeling ill, Walters was tested again. This time the mono test came back positive, confirming her case. In the meantime, she suffered through a number of symptoms. Nauseous for days, Walters found it

Sheep, Horses, and Guinea Pigs

The monospot test was developed in 1932 by Connecticut physicians John Rodman Paul and Walls Willard Bunnell. Paul and Bunnell found that when the blood of infectious mononucleosis patients was mixed with the blood of sheep and horses, the infected human cells stuck to the red cells in the blood provided by the animals. As a result, the human monocyte cells drew antibodies—which are proteins that attack diseases—from the blood of the sheep and horses.

Using animal blood to detect diseases in humans was not unusual at that time. About a decade before, researchers had determined that antibodies in animal blood could detect human diseases. The monospot test later was refined by Israel Davidsohn, a research physician at the Chicago School of Medicine, who found that human cells infected with mono bonded well with cells drawn from the kidneys of guinea pigs. The Davidsohn test found that antibodies in the blood of guinea pigs were highly accurate in detecting the presence of the Epstein-Barr virus.

impossible to eat. "I have completely lost my appetite and I have to force myself to eat," Walters says. "I can't lose any more weight."[33]

Swabbing the Throat

The initial diagnosis of Walters determined that she suffered from strep throat, which is a common mistake made by doctors in mono cases. Strep throat is spread by streptococcal bacteria. In addition to severe throat pain, streptococcal infections may cause other symptoms that are similar to mono: difficulty swallowing, swollen tonsils, swollen and tender lymph glands, fever, headache, rash, and nausea. If the doctor suspects the sore throat and other symptoms are caused by a strep infection, he or she may order a throat swab. To perform the test, the doctor or nurse will dab a sterile swab on the back of the patient's throat to capture a sample of the secretions in the throat. The swab will then be analyzed at a laboratory to determine the presence of streptococcal bacteria.

If the test comes back positive, the doctor will prescribe antibacterial drugs such as penicillin or amoxicillin. However, the test usually takes as long as three weeks to detect streptococcal bacteria since the germs have to be cultured in a petri dish. In the meantime, the doctor may direct the patient to start taking antibiotic drugs while awaiting the test results.

But what if the patient does not have strep throat and is instead suffering from mono? It means that the patient is taking antibiotic drugs for no reason. The drugs certainly will not make the patient sicker, but they will not help either. Of course, if the throat swab test comes back negative for a strep infection, it could prompt the doctor to suspect other causes, such as mono. By now, though, it is likely that the patient is still feeling ill and has returned to the doctor's office—as Walters did—and has convinced the physician that there may be another reason for the symptoms.

It is also not unusual for a patient to be suffering from both mono and strep throat. If the patient's immunity has been weakened while he or she fights off one infection, a secondary infection may have an easier time taking hold in the body.

One test that a doctor can perform that may point toward mono is known as a complete blood count (CBC). In a CBC, the doctor can tell whether the overall white blood cell count is higher than normal. The CBC test will also look at the cells that are specifically associated with the lymph nodes to see whether they are at an elevated rate. The CBC does not specifically indicate mono, but it can be helpful to doctors who may want some form of confirmation without having to wait for the week or more that it takes for the monocyte test to show results. The results of a CBC are usually available to the doctor the day following the test.

Fooled by the Symptoms

Mono patients generally recover from their illness without the help of drugs. So being misdiagnosed with strep throat or another disease will not usually cause harm. They may take some unnecessary drugs, but they will eventually get better. Of much more concern, though, is the patient who truly does have another illness but is misdiagnosed with mono. Sometimes, the monospot test may provide a "false positive," meaning it indicates the presence of mono in a patient who is suffering from another disease. For example, monospot tests have wrongly indicated mono in patients suffering from chicken pox, hepatitis, and lupus.

Chicken pox, which is spread by a herpes virus, is relatively minor if contracted by young children. In fact, parents have been known to stage "chicken pox parties," letting toddlers play with a friend who has contracted the disease so that their young children can be exposed to the virus at a time when it least affects them. In teens and adults, chicken pox can develop into the disease known as shingles, which can include a rash, blisters, and numbing pain that can last for years. Hepatitis is a viral infection spread by body fluids and fecal matter in unsanitary conditions. Its main symptom is an enlargement of the liver. Lupus is an autoimmune disease that attacks the

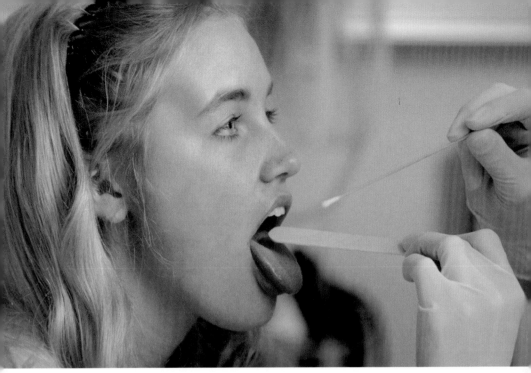

A health-care professional swabs the throat of a young girl for a culture in a strep throat test.

body's healthy tissue and organs. Treatments that can cure or minimize the severity of the symptoms in all those diseases are available, but if left untreated, they can lead to debilitating consequences and even death. Therefore, if the doctor is convinced that the patient has contracted mono, he or she will simply advise bed rest. Meanwhile, the symptoms of these diseases can grow worse and severely impact the health of the patient.

Lyme Disease

One disease that has often fooled doctors into believing their patients suffer from mono is Lyme disease. The illness was first diagnosed in 1975 in Lyme, Connecticut, and a number of neighboring communities, which is how the disease acquired its name. It is a bacterial infection spread by the bite of the deer tick. In most cases, the bite will leave a rash in the shape of a bull's-eye—a sure indication that the patient has contracted Lyme disease. However, in some cases the rash may be hard to find or it may fade or completely disappear. Some patients do not develop the rash. In the meantime, the patient manifests a number of symptoms that mimic mono, most notably relentless fatigue. Lyme disease should be treated with antibiotic drugs, but if the doctor is convinced the patient has contracted mono, then the Lyme symptoms will continue to sicken the patient while he or she tries in vain to shake them off simply by staying in bed.

In one case, a doctor advised Paula Gesmundo of Hamilton, Massachusetts, to treat her two sons' mono with aspirin. For months, the boys lived with symptoms that seemed to improve, then would grow worse, then would fade again. Finally, after their conditions failed to improve on a consistent basis, Gesmundo found a new doctor who reexamined the boys and this time determined they had contracted Lyme disease. In the meantime, the boys suffered for months through bouts of fatigue and other symptoms, including headaches, nausea, joint pain, fever, rashes, enlarged lymph glands, dif-

Deer ticks (shown in a greatly magnified microscopic image) transmit Lyme disease to humans.

ficulty sleeping, night sweats, occasional loss of vision, and difficulty concentrating. Since their Lyme disease progressed as far as it did with no treatment, the boys have had to remain on antibiotic drugs for a much longer period than normal. The Gesmundos have been forced to spend thousands of dollars on drugs and make frequent visits to the doctor's office. "I cannot tell you what has become of our lives,"[34] says Paula Gesmundo.

Rare Diseases

One consistent complaint among Lyme disease sufferers is that few doctors truly understand the disease or are aware of its symptoms, and that is why they frequently misdiagnose it as mono or other ailments. Indeed, patients who have contracted far more obscure illnesses face the same likelihood of misdiagnosis. For example, Melissa Howard, a fourteen-year-old from Lancaster, Pennsylvania, found herself suffering from intense and relentless fatigue. She was so sick that she would often pass out in the hallway at school. Occasionally, her parents dropped her off at a school dance or other event, then received a phone call from their daughter a few minutes later telling them to pick her up because she was too exhausted to stay. Originally diagnosed with mono, Melissa spent weeks in bed, wondering when her pesky infection would clear up. "It was so hard being young and having to lay in bed some days," she says. "I just wanted to be a normal teenager and not have to worry about my health."[35]

Finally, her parents refused to accept the diagnosis of mono and started looking for other answers. After numerous visits to several doctors, Melissa was finally given a correct diagnosis. She was suffering from dysautonomia, a nerve disorder that causes exhaustion and episodes of fainting. Although there is no cure for dysautonomia, there are drugs available to help the patients endure the symptoms. Melissa has also been taking nutritional supplements, which have helped her find new sources of energy and maintain more of a typical teen's life.

Another rare disease that has been confused for mono is histiocytosis, a genetic condition that strikes one in two hundred thousand people, mostly children under the age of ten but many adolescents and adults as well. Histiocytosis is similar to cancer because rogue cells form into tumors. It is known to produce a skin rash as well as swollen lymph nodes and to attack the liver and spleen, which are all common symptoms of mono. In some patients, the disease clears up on its own and treatments are not needed. In others, though, the disease can be as resilient as cancer and require extensive treatments. Patients who have developed histiocytosis may have to undergo chemotherapy and radiation therapy to destroy the rogue cells in their bodies, a long and often difficult process that underscores the fact that histiocytosis is a far more serious ailment than mono.

Sharing Symptoms with Leukemia

Histiocytosis is not a form of cancer, but one type of cancer, leukemia, has at times been misdiagnosed as mono. Leukemia is a cancer of the blood and bone marrow that breaks down the patient's immunity to other diseases. It can be a particularly devastating disease, lasting for many years. Patients often have to endure long and unpleasant treatments involving chemotherapy. Severe cases of leukemia may require bone marrow transplants. Certainly, leukemia can be fatal and is a major cause of death in children and young adults who suffer from the disease.

Leukemia patients exhibit high fevers and other flulike symptoms; fatigue; enlarged lymph glands, livers, and spleens; and swollen tonsils. Also, leukemia can be diagnosed through a high white cell count, which is also an indicator of mono. In fact, the symptoms of the two diseases are so similar that in the first few decades following the discovery of glandular fever by Emil Pfeiffer, physicians often had difficulty telling the difference between the two.

Essentially, the only accurate way physicians could diagnose leukemia was to wait and see whether the glandular

Does the Patient Own a Cat?

If a physician asks a patient whether he or she owns a cat, the doctor may be interested in more than just friendly conversation about felines. In fact, the doctor may suspect that the patient has contracted toxoplasmosis, a disease with symptoms very similar to those of infectious mononucleosis.

The disease is spread by a parasite known as *Toxoplasma gondii* that is found in cat feces. The parasite can be ingested by the cat owner, who may not thoroughly wash his or her hands after cleaning the litter box. The parasite can also be found in pork, lamb, and deer meat and can be ingested if the meat is not cooked thoroughly.

Patients who contract toxoplasmosis may develop flulike symptoms as well as swollen lymph glands, aches, and pains that can last a month or more. Toxoplasmosis is frequently misdiagnosed as mono because, in many patients, the disease causes an enlargement of the liver and spleen. In people with healthy immune systems, the symptoms usually clear up by themselves after the body's natural defenses eradicate the parasite. People with weaker immune systems may be given antibiotic drugs to help their bodies destroy the parasite. As for the cat, in most cases the animal's immune system will eradicate the parasite within a few weeks of being infected.

fever symptoms of their patients persisted after a few weeks. In the meantime, their nervous patients fretted over the possibility that they had contracted a potentially life-threatening disease.

At the time, blood tests provided inconclusive evidence. Under a microscope, the white blood cells that were summoned by the body to fight glandular fever appeared similar to the cells that were infected by leukemia. A breakthrough occurred in 1920, when physicians Thomas P. Sprunt and

Frank A. Evans, who were conducting a study of six glandular fever patients at Johns Hopkins University in Baltimore, discovered that the monocyte cells present in glandular fever cases grew out of the lymph glands whereas the leukemia-infected cells grew out of bone marrow. (In the article they wrote for a medical journal outlining their discovery, Sprunt and Evans referred to glandular fever as *mononucleosis*. It is believed to be the first official use of the term to describe the disease.)

Far from Foolproof

Sprunt and Evans devised a process for telling the difference between mono and leukemia. Yet because the physical symptoms of the two diseases are very similar, doctors were still fooled. Later, the development of the monospot test further assisted doctors in diagnosing mono. However, even now, with the assistance of the monospot test as well as tests that can detect the presence of cancer in the body, doctors realize that tests are sometimes fallible. They are aware that there is a remote possibility that mono patients may, in fact, be suffering from leukemia.

Pop singer Rich Cronin was initially told that he had contracted mononucleosis. In 2001 Cronin and his group, LFO, recorded the hit single "Summer Girls." After the group broke up, Cronin hoped to start a solo career. By early 2005 he had been working hard on an album when he started feeling ill. "I started to feel tired when I would walk up stairs, and I would start getting pretty sharp headaches," Cronin says. "But I never thought much of it, because I had always been a pretty healthy guy."[36]

Cronin finally visited a clinic, where he was examined and diagnosed with a viral infection. "They just told me to let it run its course,"[37] Cronin says. Two weeks later, still feeling ill, Cronin saw another doctor, who suggested mono but urged him to undergo additional tests. When the results of the new tests were analyzed, they indicated the singer had contracted leukemia.

Cronin has undergone chemotherapy treatments, and his leukemia is in remission. Nevertheless, he still fears for his life. "I'm scared to death at this point," he admits. "It's a nightmare of a situation to be in, but I really want to make something positive out of this."[38]

Cronin's case shows that more than a hundred years after Pfeiffer's discovery, mononucleosis remains a mysterious

Teen heartthrob Rich Cronin, formerly of LFO, was finally diagnosed with leukemia after doctors initially suspected mono.

and often misdiagnosed disease. The symptoms of other diseases often mimic those of mono, fooling doctors. Moreover, the main test for mono, the monospot test, is far from foolproof. False negative tests often prompt doctors to search for other causes for the fatigue, fevers, and sore throats that plague their patients. At the same time, patients find themselves wondering why their doctors cannot seem to tell them what is wrong.

CHAPTER FOUR

Living with Infectious Mononucleosis

It seems that during every semester, somebody in a dormitory somewhere on a college campus in the United States comes down with a case of infectious mononucleosis. Campus health center officials are accustomed to seeing multiple cases of mono each semester. Such outbreaks are not due to epidemics in which the disease spreads rapidly through the community. Rather, the lifestyle of most American college students—living in dormitories, spending long hours in study, going to parties late at night, neglecting personal hygiene—makes them prime candidates for contracting mono.

As college students—as well as other mono patients—suffer through the illness, many are shocked to find that there are no wonder drugs that can make their sickness go away. Although doctors may prescribe drugs to ease some of the symptoms, the only way for a mono sufferer to start feeling better is to get plenty of rest and let the disease run its course. But asking a college student to stay in bed for a couple of weeks may jeopardize his or her grades; many students find it difficult to miss two weeks of classes and still pass their courses. As a result, many students find no alternative but to drop out of school for a semester. As Luke Beno, a pediatrician in Jonesboro, Arkansas, explains, "The older the child, the longer the infection takes to heal, sometimes as long as three months. Some kids with mono become so fatigued that they have to drop out of school and extracurricular activities until their strength returns."[39]

Most unfortunate are those mono sufferers who go on to develop chronic fatigue syndrome (CFS). Medical research is continuing to show the links between the Epstein-Barr virus (EBV) and CFS. Indeed, CFS sufferers may be facing years of relentless fatigue and other troubling symptoms, making it difficult for them to carve out productive lives. Some CFS sufferers do find a way to overcome their diseases. Laura Hillenbrand was diagnosed with EBV as a college sophomore. Despite suffering for years with CFS, she was able to muster the energy to write the best-selling book *Seabiscuit: An American Legend.* The book tells the story of Seabiscuit, the castoff thoroughbred that went on to become a champion racehorse in the 1930s. In 2003 the book was adapted into the Academy Award–winning film *Seabiscuit.* Hillenbrand says, "As I lay in bed over the years, I wished that somebody prominent would go out and make an

Statistics About Infectious Mononucleosis and EBV

Infection by Mononucleosis and EBV	Statistic
In the U.S., how many adults between 35–40 years of age have been infected by infectious mononucleosis and/or EBV?	95%
How many adults infected with EBV will **not** develop symptoms of infectious mononucleosis?	80%
When infection with EBV occurs during adolescence or young adulthood, how often does it cause infectious mononucleosis?	35–50% of diagnosed cases of EBV will end up with infectious mononucleosis

Taken from: National Center for Infectious Diseases
Available online at: http://www.cdc.gov/ncidod/diseases/ebv.htm

Because college students often live in close quarters, diseases such as mono can easily infect a large group.

articulate case for CFS patients. So when *Seabiscuit*'s success gave me the opportunity to take on that role, I thought, OK, that's what I'm going to try to do."[40]

Hectic Lifestyles

In the fall of 2007, health officials at the University of Tennessee at Chattanooga reported twenty cases of mono on campus. Meanwhile, at Ball State University in Indiana, staff members at the campus health center found themselves treating no fewer than fifteen mono cases a week. And at Oklahoma Christian University, health center staff members were stunned in 2006 by the number of students who contracted the infection. "We have at least, I would guess, at least a dozen people right now that we know of that are in some either acute or recovery phase since school started through the last couple of weeks," health center director Pamela Ferguson says. "And I'm sure there's more we haven't seen or have gone off campus. But last week we had three new ones and probably that many this week."[41]

Natural Sore Throat Remedies

Sore throat remedies are not only found in the medicine cabinet but also in the kitchen cabinet.

Experts in herbal medicine believe that a number of spices and roots can have a soothing effect on a sore throat. For example, they recommend that gargling with a mixture of tea and ginger root can help reduce the inflammation of a sore throat. Another gargle that can help make a sore throat feel better can be made by mixing a teaspoon of cinnamon into a cup of water, hot or cold. Cinnamon contains mucilage, an ingredient that will coat the throat and ease the inflammation.

Cayenne, which is also known as red pepper, can be used as a gargle as well. To make the gargle, herbal experts suggest mixing an eighth of a teaspoon of cayenne with freshly squeezed lemon juice and a pinch of salt.

Licorice root also has a soothing effect on an achy throat. "It's sweet, has a nice coating action and it treats the inflammation," says Karta Purkh Singh Khalsa, a Seattle, Washington, herbal medicine expert and the author of the book *Herbal Defense*. To ease a sore throat, Khalsa recommends drinking two cups a day of hot water containing a tablespoon of ground licorice root.

Quoted in Norine Dworkin, "Sore Throat Relief," *Vegetarian Times*, October 1998, p. 94.

It is not unusual for mono to sweep through a college campus. For starters, students who reside in dormitories live in close quarters, where there are many opportunities to be infected. These include tiny dorm rooms, communal bathrooms, cafeterias, and even lecture halls where hundreds of students may gather for their classes and where their coughs and sneezes waft through the windowless rooms. Moreover, for many students college is an opportunity to enjoy the types of freedoms they may not have known at home. There are many opportunities to go to parties, where drinks, straws, cigarettes, or other substances may be shared by many people. College romances may blossom; sometimes, casual relationships may suddenly turn romantic. According to Chris Smith, the director of the student health center at the University of Tennessee, "People are not vigilant in keeping their bodily fluids to themselves."[42]

In addition, it is not unusual for some students to put off their studies until shortly before tests or due dates for reports and papers. In the meantime, they go to parties. Then, as their deadlines approach, they work around the clock to keep their grades up. This type of hectic lifestyle can place a lot of stress on their bodies and helps break down their immune systems, making it harder to fight off infections, particularly mono.

Freshmen are among the most likely students to contract mono. They are new to the college lifestyle, and many have not learned how to balance the demands of schoolwork against the time they spend on social activities. As Beverly Beckwith, the director of nursing for the University of Connecticut, explains, "Stress levels increase sharply, especially for freshmen. They are out on their own—many for the first time—and they have no structure in their lives. They have fatigue. They may not be eating right because they're skipping dorm meals. They're living close to other students. Some are homesick. They need some structure in their lives."[43]

At Oklahoma Christian, freshman Robby Coles admits that his poor dietary habits as well as his lack of sleep contributed to his bout of mono, which forced him to miss a month of classes and even spend a brief period in the hospital. Back on campus, Coles says he has made a commitment to leading a healthier lifestyle. "I've started drinking more water, not skipping any meals, and sleeping when my body told me it was time," he says. "I'm not going to force myself to stay awake for school work anymore. My health is worth more than a degree. I want to do well here, but I need to make sure I am OK first."[44]

Another Oklahoma Christian student, Josh Rose, missed fifteen classes while recovering from mono. "It's basically murder on my grades," he says. "You don't really have the energy to stay awake, let alone focus on homework. But the teachers are willing to work with you. It's a 'when you get it done, turn it in' type of thing. If the teachers wouldn't have been willing to work with me it would have been very difficult."[45]

Missing Classes

While most mono sufferers must spend time in recovery, the severity of their symptoms varies and, therefore, dictates how long it will take them to return to their normal schedules. Certainly, someone with just modest symptoms may be able to rise out of bed after a short period of time and attend classes or do other activities, albeit probably at something of a slower pace. For example, Colorado State University freshman Paul Klinger missed most of his classes for a week but still found the energy to drag himself to his course in Japanese, mostly because he had a project due that week. "I had to do a presentation,"[46] he says.

On the other hand, a young person or other patient who suffers through severe mono symptoms may have a much more difficult time getting back to normal. At Ball State, one of Lauren Schmidt's symptoms was a severely swollen spleen, which could have been a potentially life-threatening condition if it had ruptured. As a result, it took Schmidt a month to recover from mono. During her recovery, until her spleen returned to normal, Schmidt could do no activities that would have placed her in jeopardy of being bumped in the abdomen. And so she missed a month's worth of classes and found herself sleeping ten hours a night. "I made sure I got enough sleep,"[47] Schmidt says.

While enduring their episodes of mono, Schmidt, Coles, and Rose managed to stay in school and, despite missing classes and falling behind in their schoolwork, still completed their semesters. Other students suffering from mono are not able to keep up with their studies. Many students fall so far behind that they have no choice but to drop out of school for the semester and return home. Eric Thompson, a senior at the University of Tennessee at Chattanooga, says he became so ill that he had to drop

Students living with mono find themselves with little energy to deal with schoolwork and may fall far behind their peers.

out of school. "It was hard to do homework and be motivated," he explains. "All I wanted to do was sleep all the time."[48]

Thompson found university officials sympathetic to his plight. He was able to withdraw from classes without receiving failing grades, which preserved his scholarship. For the following semester, he resumed his studies and eventually graduated, although he received his diploma a few months later than he had originally anticipated.

As for Colorado State University student Zeb Carabello, he did not have to miss classes when he contracted mono. Carabello hardly considered himself lucky, though. Carabello came down with mono during spring break. He did not fall behind on his schoolwork, but he also did not get to take a much-anticipated trip to Arizona, where he planned to spend his vacation amid palm trees, attending poolside parties. Instead, Carabello spent spring break mostly on the sofa in his parents' home, nursing a painfully sore throat. "The inevitable happened," he says. "I got mono."[49]

No Magic Bullet

When Coles, Rose, Klinger, and the other mono patients checked themselves into their campus health centers or saw their own doctors, they likely received the rather depressing news that there was no magic bullet that would make them get better. Penicillin and other antibiotic drugs have no effect on mono. Therefore, mono patients are advised to get plenty of rest and wait for the illness to go away on its own.

However, there are some medications and home remedies that can help mono patients feel better by making the symptoms less severe. For starters, physicians always counsel their patients to drink plenty of fluids, particularly water, tea, and fruit juices. These fluids can help prevent the dehydration that may accompany high fevers. A patient can also become dehydrated by not eating regularly, which typically occurs during a bout with mono, or by repeated vomiting, which afflicts many mono patients.

When patients become dehydrated, they may experience headaches, dizziness, low blood pressure, and other ill effects. In other words, dehydration can make mono symptoms even more severe. "To prevent dehydration, be sure you drink enough fluids," advises Barton D. Schmitt, a professor of pediatrics at the University of Colorado School of Medicine. "Milk shakes and cold drinks are especially good. You can also sip warm chicken broth."[50] According to Schmitt, the warning signs of dehydration include a mouth that lacks saliva or is otherwise dry, urine that is darker than normal, and urination that occurs fewer than three times a day.

The severe headaches that often afflict mono patients can be made less painful by taking painkillers such as ibuprofen or acetaminophen. Both are also effective in reducing fever and relieving the achy feelings suffered by most mono patients, particularly the soreness they feel in their lymph glands. Patients under twenty are advised not to take aspirin without a doctor's approval. In young patients, aspirin that is used to treat viral infections is suspected of sparking Reye's syndrome, a disease that attacks the brain and liver.

There are many remedies for sore throat pain as well. Certainly, there are dozens of varieties of throat lozenges available in pharmacies that can help ease throat pain, but some mono patients may not even need to make a trip to the drug store. Some doctors recommend eating frozen desserts or drinking cold beverages to ease throat pain. Doctors also recommend gargling with a solution of a half teaspoon of salt mixed into a glass of warm water. Sucking on hard candies is also recommended to help ease sore throat pain. Some people find that drinking a mixture of hot tea and honey will make their throats feel better. In cases of severe sore throats that threaten to block the air supply to the lungs, doctors may order their patients to take prescription anti-inflammatory drugs to reduce the swelling.

Since mono often robs patients of their appetites, Schmitt recommends that they take doses of multiple vitamins until their appetites return. If patients are hungry, but they find it difficult to swallow, Schmitt suggests eating soft foods, such as ice cream, gelatin desserts, broths, or soups.

Mono patients who have enlarged spleens should take precautions to ensure that they do not become constipated. A person who is constipated may place stress on his or her abdomen during a bowel movement. To avoid constipation, people should drink plenty of fluids and eat fruits and vegetables. Daily consumption of a glass of water containing a fiber supplement can also help a mono patient avoid constipation.

Living with CFS

For people who suffer from chronic fatigue syndrome, no amount of acetaminophen, ibuprofen, tea and honey, or bed rest seems to make them feel better. Indeed, CFS has stumped doctors for decades. There is no known cure for the ailment, nor is there an effective treatment that seems to work for everybody. Instead, CFS sufferers often find out, through trial and error, what works best for them.

Many CFS sufferers soon learn the limits of their endurance. They know, for example, that they may be able to mow the lawn, but additional yard work performed on the same day

A woman overcome with chronic fatigue syndrome lies on her bed, close to the many medications she must take.

will wear them out. They may limit themselves to one errand outside the home a day. Some CFS patients have a hard time shaking cold symptoms. Their runny noses, scratchy throats, and coughs may last weeks or even months. As a result, they tend to stay home and have little contact with others during the winter or at other times of the year if they hear that some of their friends may be suffering from cold symptoms.

One symptom of CFS that many patients must endure is the so-called brain fog. They find themselves unable to concentrate—a truly frightening symptom that sometimes occurs even during periods in which they otherwise feel fine. CFS patient Linda Dooley says, "Not being able to get out of bed to fix breakfast for your children is humiliating, but you are terrified of being crazy when you can't remember how to (drive) the car or you can't remember where you are or where you were headed."[51] Dooley's husband, Robert, says he could see his wife's frustration at not being able to lead a normal life. "I knew Linda wanted to work and wanted to have a social life," he says. "I saw her crying over her frustration of not being able to do what she wanted. I knew she was trying. I knew she was not crazy."[52]

Still, many CFS patients do find ways to lead productive lives. Laura Hillenbrand had been a tennis player, horseback rider, competitive swimmer, and straight-A student when, as a college student in Ohio, she suddenly felt sick. Hillenbrand had eaten in a restaurant earlier that day and believed she had been made ill by the food. Most food poisoning cases pass in a few hours or days, but Hillenbrand's nausea and weakness lasted for several weeks. "Even if the building had been burning down, I wouldn't have been able to get out of bed,"[53] she recalls.

Finally, Hillenbrand was forced to withdraw from her classes and return home to Maryland, where she tried to recover. It took two years for her to feel well enough to work again. In the meantime, she saw seven doctors and was finally diagnosed with CFS.

She found some part-time work as a freelance writer, then suffered a relapse and was once again confined to bed. It was during this second phase of home confinement in which Hillenbrand learned about thoroughbred racehorse Seabiscuit and devoted herself to writing the story of the unlikely champion.

Hillenbrand spent four years writing the book in the throes of CFS. She had to adapt her work schedule to her illness, sometimes keeping food by her bed so that she would not waste energy walking to the kitchen. At times she had to rest after taking a shower in the morning; the physical effort of standing for just a few minutes under the shower wore her out. When she could not get out of bed, she wrote in longhand. She would sometimes have to do so with her eyes closed to avoid the dizziness that afflicts CFS sufferers. Working through the illness, Hillenbrand managed to conduct some 150 interviews by phone and transcribed each interview herself.

Mono Helped Launch His Career

Most people do not regard infectious mononucleosis as a positive experience, but for Adam Kee the illness helped him choose his career path. Kee, a New York–based actor, was active in sports in his hometown of Johnston City, Illinois, but when he was in junior high school he contracted mono.

While recovering from mono, Kee's doctor told him he could not play sports. Instead, Kee tried out for the school play—and got the part. "I played sports when I was younger. I guess I was OK since they let me put a jersey on," he says. "After [getting mono in] the sixth grade, I got the [acting] bug and started doing eight or nine shows a year."

Kee was educated at the Actors Studio in New York, where he has assisted in the production of the Bravo network's *Inside the Actors Studio*. He has also won a role on the TV drama *Law and Order* and has appeared in a number of New York stage productions.

Quoted in Matt Hawkins, "New York Actor Kee Returns to His Hometown for the Holidays," *Marion Daily Republican*, December 26, 2007. www.mariondaily.com/articles/2007/12/26/news/news01.txt.

As she worked on the book, she realized that the story of Seabiscuit was similar to her own story. The book tells the story of an owner, Charles Howard; a trainer, Tom Smith; and a jockey, Red Pollard, who overcame tremendous adversities in their own lives to achieve success. "Here was a story I could get lost in," she says. "Writing [*Seabiscuit*] helped me redefine myself, to become Laura the author instead of Laura the sick person. That was very rewarding."[54]

Seabiscuit, which was published in 2001, became a critical and commercial success, but in writing the book Hillenbrand paid a deep price. Shortly after completing the manuscript, Hillenbrand suffered a relapse. She was forced to return to bed, troubled by the chronic dizziness that afflicts many CFS sufferers. Hillenbrand admits, "I absolutely destroyed myself in finishing *Seabiscuit*."[55]

A Courageous Battle

In the years since the publication of *Seabiscuit* and its adaptation into a major motion picture, Hillenbrand has regained her health somewhat. In 2004 she felt well enough to begin work on a second book—a biography of Louis Zamperini, a track-and-field competitor at the 1936 Olympics. As a U.S. Air Force bombardier during World War II, Zamperini's plane was shot down over the Pacific Ocean. He survived in a life raft and then, after his rescue by the Japanese, Zamperini spent two years in a prisoner-of-war camp. As with her work on *Seabiscuit*, though, Hillenbrand has been forced to make concessions to her illness while writing Zamperini's story. "My illness doesn't ever go away," she says. "Lately, things have been reasonably stable, and I have been just well enough to work fairly productively on my book. The biggest obstacle remains my vertigo, which makes reading and writing an enormous struggle. There are days during which I can't work because of it, but most days I can get something done."[56]

Hillenbrand has waged a courageous battle against her CFS symptoms. Certainly, though, most infectious mononucleosis cases do not develop into CFS. Most young people who suffer from mono will not have to worry about years of fatigue and other persistent and troubling symptoms that will alter the way they live. Indeed, most mono sufferers need only drink lots of fluids, get plenty of rest, and endure the unpleasant but temporary symptoms that will, in time, go away on their own.

CHAPTER FIVE

Avoiding Infectious Mononucleosis

Although infectious mononucleosis is not easily transmitted from person to person, people would be foolish to assume they are safe and should not take precautions. In fact, there are many safeguards people can take to help keep the risks of contracting mono to a minimum.

Physicians believe that maintaining good hygiene is at the top of the list. Not sharing drinks or eating utensils with others and washing hands often can help guard against the spread of viral infections. Getting plenty of sleep and exercise and eating a healthy diet can help maintain a strong immune system, which is vital to fighting off viral infections. "We do know that stress and fatigue compromise the immune system and we also know, for a fact, that it makes you susceptible to a whole range of other conditions,"[57] says Caesar Briefer, the director of health services at the University of Michigan.

In the years since Michael Epstein and Yvonne Barr identified the virus that causes mono, a search has been conducted for a vaccine that would wipe out the Epstein-Barr virus (EBV) as well as cytomegalovirus (CMV). Although there have been recent developments that appear to be promising, there does not appear to be any near-term hope that a vaccine will be made available to prevent people from contracting mono as well as many other diseases that are sparked by EBV and CMV. Until a vaccine is discovered, people would be wise to use some common sense when it comes to protecting themselves against germs.

Avoiding the "Freshman Fifteen"

Young people who go away to college and live on their own for the first time discover a treasure trove of junk food. Pizza shops, coffee bars, and fast-food restaurants line the main streets through campus; sidewalk vendors grill up midday snacks that can be munched between classes; and vending machines in the lobbies of classroom buildings dispense candy, iced cupcakes, soft drinks, and other treats. When the students return home for winter break, they may find they have gained some weight—the "freshman fifteen," which are the 15 or so pounds (6.8kg) they gained by eating fatty foods. "The 'freshman 15,' an almost universal phenomenon, happens when people who have been eating fairly sensible, balanced diets suddenly have too much freedom to snarf late-night pizza, fries with every meal, and the daily ice cream from the 'build-your-own-sundae-bar' in the dining hall," explains Janet Farrar Worthington, author of the *Ultimate College Survival Guide*. "The result: Until they figure out how to eat right, they blimp up into the chunky little Pillsbury dough people."[58]

Eating the wrong foods does more than just add weight to a student's middle. A steady diet of junk food can help weaken an immune system, which can make a person more susceptible to viral infections, including mono. "Nutrition plays an important part in maintaining immune function," says George L. Blackburn, associate director of the division of nutrition at Harvard Medical School in Massachusetts. "Insufficiency in one or more essential nutrients may prevent the immune system from functioning at its peak."[59]

A healthy diet helps manufacture white blood cells, which are the body's natural infection fighters. Diets rich in vitamins A and C, which are found in fruits and vegetables, are particularly

Giving in to the temptation of junk food like chips and candy may weaken the immune system.

effective in white blood cell production. Such foods are important sources of antioxidants, the chemicals that remove harmful oxidants from the bloodstream. Oxidants, also known as free radicals, are the toxic by-products left over after the body converts food into energy. Free radicals also enter the body through cigarette smoke, pollution, ultraviolet radiation from the sun, and other environmental sources. Free radicals are believed to enhance the onset of some diseases. Having a healthy supply of antioxidants in the body does not prevent disease, but it helps the body fight off infection. To furnish the body with an adequate supply of antioxidants, health experts recommend eating between five and nine fruits and vegetables a day.

Among the best sources of antioxidants are prunes, raisins, blueberries, blackberries, strawberries, raspberries, plums, oranges, red grapes, cherries, kiwi fruit, pink grapefruits, kale, spinach, brussels sprouts, alfalfa sprouts, broccoli, beets, red bell peppers, onions, corn, and eggplant. According to Worthington, "When your mom told you to eat your vegetables, she probably didn't mean French fries and onion rings."[60]

Also, white blood cells thrive on proteins, which also help give the body energy—an important consideration for somebody battling against the relentless fatigue of mono. Sources of protein include lean fish, seafood, poultry, eggs, lentils, beans, and soy products. Blackburn advises, "Cover two-thirds of your plate with vegetables, fruit, whole grains, and beans, and one-third with lean protein."[61]

Healthy Habits

Exercise is also an important way to keep the immune system healthy. Studies have shown that exercise can enhance the production of infection-fighting white blood cells. Even just twenty or thirty minutes of brisk walking five times a week can help bolster a person's immunity against disease. Indeed, young people have plenty of opportunities to exercise in school and at home. Today, many public schools as well as colleges have realized the importance of providing fitness facilities to students and have invested in fitness centers featuring cardiovascular and strength-training equipment. Of course, it is up to the student to find the time and make the commitment to work out regularly. Worthington says, "Every little bit helps even if it's just taking the stairs instead of the elevator, or jogging up and down the halls of your dorm, or [exercising in] your room for ten minutes a night."[62]

Exercise can also help reduce stress, which can contribute to a weaker immune system. People who are under stress or anxiety or in a panic—it may be Sunday night and they are just getting started on term papers that are due Monday morning—often compromise their immune systems. In this case, the best

A Cerebral Cure for Chronic Fatigue Syndrome

Some health experts believe the cure for chronic fatigue syndrome patients may be found in their brains rather than in their bodies. Laura Hillenbrand, for one, sees a psychologist in an effort to come to terms with the physical stress the disease has put on her body.

The author of *Seabiscuit: An American Legend*, Hillenbrand has suffered from CFS since she was a college sophomore. She spent many years confined to bed as she endured CFS. She believes that many CFS patients may compound their illnesses by letting the disease affect their mental health. The years of fatigue and pain force them into downward spirals of anxiety and depression.

"We're talking about how I'm perceiving the illness and what my expectations are," Hillenbrand says of the sessions with her therapist. "I don't think I went into the illness with these problems, but over the years of being traumatized by Chronic Fatigue Syndrome, you develop problems that make it harder for you to recover from it. I'm feeling better, and I think ultimately the treatment will help me."

Quoted in Larry Katzenstein, "Betting on Seabiscuit," *Smithsonian*, December 2002, p. 58.

way to avoid stress is to get a head start on schoolwork and not scramble to meet deadlines at the last minute.

There are many other causes of stress in a young person's life. Relationship problems, for example, can evolve into a major source of stress. Friends sometimes get angry with one another. Boyfriends and girlfriends have fights and break up. Experts on stress counsel young people to stay calm and accept a change in a relationship as part of life. Also, a brisk jog around the running track or thirty minutes on the treadmill at the fitness center may also help calm the nerves.

Losing sleep over a breakup with a boyfriend or girlfriend can help weaken an immune system. In fact, losing sleep for any reason, such as staying up late to go to parties or studying into the early hours of the morning, can prove detrimental to a person's ability to fight off an infection. "Teens are chronically sleep-deprived and a lot of times they are stressed, and their immune system is less able to fight [the infection] off,"[63] says Delaware pediatrician Barbara Homeier.

Of course, even a person who exercises regularly, gets plenty of sleep, learns to handle stress, and maintains a healthy diet can contract mono. Chances are, though, that somebody with a healthy immune system will suffer symptoms that are relatively mild. He or she will more likely be back to a normal routine a lot quicker than somebody who does not exercise, sacrifices sleep, and eats a steady diet of pizza, chocolate bars, and cheeseburgers.

Staying Out of the "Hot Zone"

Another way to keep the body healthy is to stay away from germs. Some of the best ways to avoid mono can be employed simply by using common sense. People should not share drinks, straws, or eating utensils. High schools and colleges are often places where students first experiment with alcohol, tobacco, and marijuana use—habits that should be avoided at all costs anyway, but made worse if the students share cups of beer or inhale from each other's cigarettes.

In recent years a game known as "beer pong" has swept across many college campuses. To play the game, two teams try to bounce Ping Pong balls into cups of beer set up at each end of a table. If one team scores a hit, the defending team must drink the beer in the cup. By the end of the game, it is likely that the members of each team have put their lips against numerous cups. Some players acknowledge the health risks and try not to share cups. But they admit that once the game gets under way it can be difficult to remember who used which

During spring break, university students play beer pong. Such games encourage the spread of mono and other diseases.

cup, especially since their judgments have been impaired by alcohol. At Bryn Mawr College in Pennsylvania, one student told the school newspaper, "I have gotten sick from sharing cups in beer pong."[64]

Parties are not the only places where germs congregate. While eating in the high school cafeteria, sitting in the bleachers at the basketball game, or studying together in the school library, students may find themselves in the pathway of germs that cause viral infections. Teammates should not share the same water bottles. A student living in a dormitory should not let someone borrow his or her toothbrush, towel, or razor. People should be wary of roommates or classmates who appear to be ill because they can easily spread viral infections through their sneezes or coughs. Michael Deichen, the associate director of student health at the University of South

Florida in Orlando, suggests staying out of an ill person's "hot zone"—the 3-foot-long (0.9m) distance that saliva or mucus can travel after a sneeze or cough. "Your risk of mono and most upper respiratory illnesses is diminished by staying out of the hot zone of an ill person and maintaining good hand hygiene,"[65] he says.

Deichen recommends frequent hand washing at all times, not just when people are around others who may appear to be ill. People who have not been exposed to EBV or CMV who do not wash their hands regularly increase the chances of ingesting the virus by putting their fingers in their mouths or touching their noses or eyes—places where viral infections often enter the body.

Searching for a Vaccine

Regardless of how well someone washes his or her hands or takes other precautions, mono can still strike. Once the patient gets over the mono, it is unlikely the disease will recur. However, there are many people who have never been exposed to EBV or CMV, and the chances that they will contract mono remain a threat in their lives. For decades scientists have searched for vaccines that would shield people against EBV as well as CMV. Not only would such vaccines help people resist mono, but it is also possible that many other diseases suspected to be caused by EBV and CMV, including Guillain-Barré syndrome, multiple sclerosis, Burkitt's lymphoma, and chronic fatigue syndrome, could also be eradicated. The discovery of vaccines that could prevent EBV and CMV would mark a major milestone in medical science.

Vaccines that would prevent EBV and CMV have been elusive, but in the past few years scientists have made some promising discoveries. In the search for an effective CMV vaccine, researchers have concentrated on altering the genetic makeup of the virus. For example, in 2006 scientists at the Wistar Institute, a biomedical research foundation in Philadelphia, announced that they had discovered a form of CMV common in mice. This form of CMV is harmless to humans. Wistar scientists hope to introduce human genes into the mouse CMV, genetically altering it so that it can survive in the human body and, theoretically, create immunity to all forms of CMV.

Meanwhile, researchers at the Texas Medical Center in Houston believe they can alter EBV cells by adding proteins to them. Proteins are chemicals that give the cells structure, immunity from disease, and other qualities. Using the altered EBV cells, they hope to develop antibodies that are specifically designed to attack those proteins and, therefore, the EBV cells that host them. The research is aimed at wiping out cancers of the lymph system, but if a vaccine is developed, then mono may become a concern of the past as well.

Proteins are also being studied as a cause of chronic fatigue syndrome (CFS). In Belgium, scientists have found that patients fight off EBV by releasing certain enzymes. Enzymes are proteins that kick-start or accelerate other reactions in cells. During a bout of mono, the enzyme level in the body remains high, but once the infection is defeated, the level typically drops. The Belgian researchers have found, though, that in CFS patients the enzyme levels remain high even though the EBV infection would seem to have run its course. The Belgian researchers believe that if they can find a way to reduce the levels of the rogue enzymes, there may be hope for CFS patients. Such experiments are still in their early stages. Nevertheless, the Belgian scientists point out that until very recently most physicians and medical researchers had little understanding of what caused CFS. Now that the origins of the disease are much better understood, they say, scientists have a much better chance of finding a cure. According to Kenny De Meirleir, the lead scientist in the Belgium study, "We now have a complete understanding of the biology of CFS."[66]

A separate body of research into EBV is also under way in Belgium, where an experimental drug has been administered to patients to block a protein that is believed to facilitate the entry of the virus into the body. During an eighteen-month period, 10 percent of the patients in the ninety-one-member

Singing "Happy Birthday" Twice

Michael Deichen, the associate director of student health at the University of South Florida in Orlando, has found that many young people simply do not know how to wash their hands. According to Deichen, proper hand washing can greatly reduce the spread of viral illnesses, including infectious mononucleosis:

> Throughout the day our hands come into contact with many potentially infectious materials. Simply washing your hands before you eat, and avoiding touching your eyes, mouth or nose, will diminish your risk of illness. Preferably, you should wash your hands with warm, soapy water. Make sure to clean between your fingers and clean long enough to sing *Happy Birthday* twice."

Michael Deichen, "Fall Illness and Hand Hygiene," September 26, 2007. http://ucf healthservices.blogspot.com.

control group contracted mono; just 2 percent of the patients in the ninety-member vaccinated group contracted the disease. The research is sponsored by several Belgian hospitals and drug companies. Based on the early findings, the sponsors hope to continue the research to find an effective EBV vaccine. As Etienne M. Sokal, the lead scientist in the study, explains, "There is currently no possibility to prevent or treat acute mononucleosis, which has remained so far an unmet medical problem. This vaccine may decrease the socio-economic impact of acute mononucleosis."[67]

A Wonder Drug

While the search continues for a vaccine, medical researchers are also exploring drugs that can be used to eradicate the symptoms of mono as well as the other diseases caused by EBV and CMV. If such a wonder drug is developed, it would perform much as an antibiotic acts against strep throat and other bacterial infections. Instead of a patient spending weeks or longer in bed suffering through unpleasant symptoms,

Research indicates that the dietary supplement glucosamine sulfate, shown here, may help patients with multiple sclerosis.

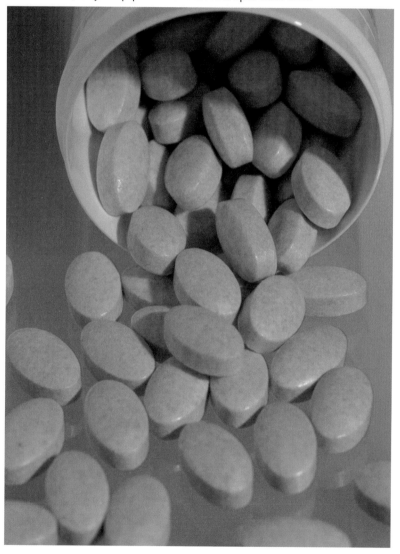

the drug could clear up the headaches, fever, swollen lymph glands, and fatigue in a matter of days.

At Stanford University in California, researchers commenced a trial of the drug valganciclovir in 2007 to determine whether it would be effective in CFS cases. In the past, valganciclovir has been administered to AIDS patients who have contracted CMV-related diseases because of their weak immune systems. Valganciclovir is a radical drug—it reduces the number of blood cells in the body. By reducing the overall blood cell count, the amount of CMV cells are reduced as well. Therefore, the virus goes away because there are not a sufficient number of viral cells in the body to support it. But the drug can produce some significant and unpleasant side effects, including anemia, which is a lack of red blood cells. Red blood cells supply oxygen to the brain and other organs. People who suffer from anemia may be fatigued and have difficulty concentrating and catching their breath. Despite the drawbacks of the drug, preliminary results from the Stanford study indicate it could hold promise as a cure for CFS. In the first trial of the drug, nine out of twelve patients said the medication helped lessen the severity of their CFS symptoms. One patient who participated in the trial was Donna Flowers of Los Gatos, California. A one-time professional figure skater, Flowers had to give up many of her physical activities due to her affliction with CFS. Six months after taking the drug, Flowers said she has taken up snowboarding, ballet lessons, and participates in a yoga class. Flowers said she still does not feel as strong as she did before she contracted CFS, but there is no question that valganciclovir has made a difference in her life. "Now I pace myself, but I'm probably 75 percent of normal,"[68] she says.

In recent years many advancements also have been made in treating multiple sclerosis (MS). As recently as the early 1990s, there were few therapies effective that could control the symptoms of the debilitating disease, but since then drugs have been developed that control MS episodes, saving patients from nerve damage, paralysis, fatigue, and other symptoms.

In addition, research has indicated that a readily available dietary supplement, glucosamine—which is extracted from soybeans—may help repair damaged nerve tissue in MS patients. So far, experiments on laboratory mice have shown that animals suffering from nerve damage have regained some ability to walk after receiving dosages of glucosamine.

As researchers develop more evidence that EBV may be at the root of MS, it is felt that some of the drugs specifically developed for multiple sclerosis patients may be effective in treating other diseases caused by EBV, including mono. "Collectively, the results . . . provide compelling evidence," says Harvard University researcher Alberto Ascherio, who has studied the relationship between MS and EBV. "I think the . . . data on MS will generate new interest in developing a vaccine [against EBV]."[69]

A Few Simple Precautions

The development of drugs that can cure infectious mononucleosis and other diseases associated with EBV and CMV are years if not decades in the future. Likewise, research into vaccines that can prevent people from contracting these diseases is also in its very early stages of development. The U.S. Food and Drug Administration (FDA), which approves all drugs and vaccines administered in America, takes many precautions before approving new medications for human consumption. All the side effects and long-term ramifications of the drug therapy must be assessed before the FDA will grant approval.

And even if the FDA does approve new drug therapies, the cure may not be pleasant. Indeed, among the side effects of valganciclovir are diarrhea, upset stomach, vomiting, loss of appetite, thirst, constipation, headache, back pain, leg swelling, and trouble walking. A chronic fatigue syndrome patient may be willing to endure those side effects to escape the relentless fatigue and pain of the disease. On the other hand, a mononucleosis patient may decide that a couple of weeks in bed with a sore throat and swollen lymph glands may be a better alternative than living through valganciclovir's side effects.

Until an effective cure or vaccine is found for mono, young people would do well to learn about the best ways to steer clear of the disease. Washing their hands, not sharing their drinking cups, staying out of the infection hot zone of an ill person, eating right, getting enough sleep, exercising, and reducing stress are some of the simple and effective precautions they can take that could truly save them from spending a few unpleasant weeks in bed.

Notes

Introduction: The Kissing Disease

1. Thomas Stuttaford, "It Started with a Kiss," *Times of London*, December 20, 2001.
2. Judith Levine Willis, "Mono," *FDA Consumer*, May/June 1998, p. 32.
3. Quoted in Ken Wunderley, "Knoch-Ed for a Loop: Outbreak of 'Mono' Hits Volleyball Team," *Pittsburgh Post-Gazette*, September 2, 2007, p. N-6.
4. Quoted in Wunderley, "Knoch-Ed for a Loop," p. N-6.
5. Quoted in Tom Fitzgerald, "Ailing Kiffin Is Back," *San Francisco Chronicle*, August 16, 2007.

Chapter One: What Is Infectious Mononucleosis?

6. Stuttaford, "It Started with a Kiss."
7. Quoted in Richard L. Carter and H.G. Penman, eds., *Infectious Mononucleosis*. Oxford, UK: Blackwell Scientific, 1969, p. 22.
8. Quoted in Willis, "Mono," p. 32.
9. Quoted in Carter and Penman, *Infectious Mononucleosis*, p. 21.
10. Quoted in Carter and Penman, *Infectious Mononucleosis*, p. 23.
11. Quoted in Carter and Penman, *Infectious Mononucleosis*, p. 40.
12. Quoted in Kirsten Weir, "Oh, No! Mono," *Current Health 2*, September 2005, p. 12.
13. Quoted in Brice Cherry, "Setbacks Have Taught BU Runner Lessons in Patience," *Waco Tribune-Herald*, October

26, 2007. www.wacotrib.com/sports/content/sports/colleg e/2007/10/26/10262007wacrunners.html.

14. Quoted in Weir, "Oh, No! Mono," p. 12.

15. Quoted in Weir, "Oh, No! Mono," p. 12.

16. Ann Japenga and Adam Overland, "The Siesta Cure," *Utne*, January/February 2004, p. 77.

17. Quoted in Carter and Penman, *Infectious Mononucleosis*, p. 40.

18. Willis, "Mono," p. 32.

Chapter Two: Can Mononucleosis Spark Other Diseases?

19. Quoted in Carter and Penman, *Infectious Mononucleosis*, p. 39.

20. Hiroshi Kimura et al., "Clinical and Virologic Characteristics of Chronic Active Epstein-Barr Virus Infection," *Blood*, July 15, 2001, p. 280.

21. Quoted in Celeste Perron, "I Used to Be a Twin," *Cosmopolitan*, December 1999, p. 228.

22. Quoted in Robert Hanley, "Cases of Rare Nerve Illness in Bergen County Puzzle Experts," *New York Times*, February 26, 1996, p. B-1.

23. Quoted in Jamie Talan, "Mono Virus Linked to MS; Strong Response to Epstein-Barr, Which Causes Mononucleosis, Seems to Double Risk of Autoimmune Disease," *Newsday*, April 12, 2006, p. A-26.

24. Quoted in William Hathaway, "Mono Virus Plays Role in Heart Disease," *Hartford Courant*, December 31, 2002, p. D-3.

25. Quoted in Carter and Penman, *Infectious Mononucleosis*, p. 228.

26. Quoted in Jesse Leavenworth, "Latest News on Chronic Fatigue: Conference Offers Insight, Hope," *Hartford Courant*, May 1, 2006, p. B-1.

27. Quoted in Danylo Hawaleshka, "Sick and So Very Tired," *Maclean's*, April 15, 2002, p. 43.

28. Quoted in Bert Wade, "'Yuppie' Disease Struggles to Get Needed Attention," *Providence Journal-Bulletin*, November 29, 1987, p. J-1.

29. Quoted in Wade, "'Yuppie' Disease Struggles to Get Needed Attention," p. J-1.

30. Quoted in David Tuller, "Chronic Fatigue No Longer Seen as 'Yuppie Flu,'" *New York Times*, July 17, 2007, p. F-6.

31. Quoted in Tuller, "Chronic Fatigue No Longer Seen as 'Yuppie Flu,'" p. F-6.

Chapter Three: A Difficult Diagnosis

32. Quoted in Willis, "Mono," p. 32.

33. Quoted in Danielle Turnbull, "Living with Mono," *Ball State University Daily News*, November 15, 2007. http://media.www.bsudailynews.com/media/storage/paper849/news/2007/11/15/Features/Living.With.Mono-3102273.shtml.

34. Quoted in Bella English, "Guess Who in This Photo Has Lyme Disease; They All Do," *Boston Globe*, June 1, 2005, p. C-6.

35. Quoted in Susan Jurgelski, "Thief of Teen Vitality: Fatigue Disorders Strike Even Society's Most Energetic," *Lancaster New Era*, August 29, 2002, p. 1.

36. Quoted in Brandee J. Tecson, "LFO Singer Rich Cronin Hospitalized with Leukemia," MTV News, April 14, 2005. www.mtv.com/news/articles/1500203/20050414/lfo.jhtml.

37. Quoted in Tecson, "LFO Singer Rich Cronin Hospitalized with Leukemia."

38. Quoted in Tecson, "LFO Singer Rich Cronin Hospitalized with Leukemia."

Chapter Four: Living with Infectious Mononucleosis

39. Luke Beno, "Prepare Kids Against Diseases in the School Environment," Kaiser Permanente news release, October 9, 2001. http://ckp.kp.org/newsroom/ga/archive/ga_011009_kids.html.

40. Quoted in Larry Katzenstein, "Betting on Seabiscuit," *Smithsonian*, December 2002, p. 58.

41. Quoted in Tracy Corcoran, "Mono Infects Many Students on Campus," *Oklahoma Christian University Talon*, November 17, 2006. http://blogs.oc.edu/ee/index.php?/talon/cat/mono_infects_many_students_on_campus.

42. Quoted in Amanda Woods, "Kissing Disease Spreads," *University of Tennessee-Chattanooga Echo*, October 4, 2007. http://media.www.utcecho.com/media/storage/paper483/news/2007/10/04/News/Kissing.Disease.Spreads-3010084.shtml.

43. Quoted in *USA Today Magazine*, "College Freedom Can Trigger Illness," December 1996, p. 6.

44. Quoted in Corcoran, "Mono Infects Many Students on Campus."

45. Quoted in Corcoran, "Mono Infects Many Students on Campus."

46. Quoted in Amy Resseguie, "Mono Makes Many Students Miss Class," *Rocky Mountain Collegian*, May 3, 2004. http://media.www.collegian.com/media/storage/paper864/news/2004/05/03/Newscampus/Mono-Makes.Students.Miss.Class-1704293.shtml.

47. Quoted in Turnbull, "Living with Mono."

48. Quoted in Woods, "Kissing Disease Spreads."

49. Zeb Carabello, "Mononucleosis, or How I Spent My Recent Vacation," *Rocky Mountain Collegian*, March 19, 2002. http://media.www.collegian.com/media/storage/paper864/news/2002/03/19/Opinion/Mononucleosis.Or.How.I.Spent.My.Recent.Vacation-1699532.shtml.

50. Barton D. Schmitt, "Infectious Mononucleosis for Teenagers," Clinical Reference Systems, January 1, 2006.

51. Quoted in Wade, "'Yuppie' Disease Struggles to Get Needed Attention," p. J-1.

52. Quoted in Wade, "'Yuppie' Disease Struggles to Get Needed Attention," p. J-1.

53. Quoted in Katzenstein, "Betting on Seabiscuit," p. 58.

54. Quoted in Katzenstein, "Betting on Seabiscuit," p. 58.

55. Quoted in Katzenstein, "Betting on Seabiscuit," p. 58.

56. Quoted in Richard Whitehead, "Against All the Odds," *Times of London*, August 6, 2005. http://entertainment. timesonline.co.uk/tol/arts_and_entertainment/books/ article551692.ece.

Chapter Five: Avoiding Infectious Mononucleosis

57. Quoted in Patricia Anstett, "Mono Is a Malady That's Mainly Misunderstood," *Albany Times Union*, November 7, 1995, p. C-1.

58. Janet Farrar Worthington, "A Healthy Student Body," *Careers and Colleges*, March/April 2005, p. 34.

59. Quoted in Stacey Colino, "Follow This Eat-Right Plan to Fortify Your Immune System," CNN.com, November 14, 2007. www.cnn.com/2007/HEALTH/diet.fitness/11/14/ cl.best.defense/index.html.

60. Worthington, "A Healthy Student Body," p. 34.

61. Quoted in Colino, "Follow This Eat-Right Plan to Fortify Your Immune System."

62. Worthington, "A Healthy Student Body," p. 34.

63. Quoted in Weir, "Oh, No! Mono," p. 12.

64. Quoted in Emily Myers, "Communal Cups Used in Beer Pong Lead to Epidemic Illness and Other Hygiene Problems," *Bi-College News*, April 25, 2006. www.biconews. com/article/view/4875.

65. Michael Deichen, "Fall Illness and Hand Hygiene," September 26, 2007. http://ucfhealthservices.blogspot.com.

66. Quoted in Hawaleshka, "Sick and So Very Tired," p. 43.

67. Quoted in *Science Daily*, "Vaccine Shows Promise in Preventing Mono," December 11, 2007. www.sciencedaily.com/releases/2007/12/071210121632.htm.

68. Quoted in Tuller, "Chronic Fatigue No Longer Seen as 'Yuppie Flu,'" p. F-6.

69. Quoted in Marie McCullough, "MS Treatment: Hope for Vaccine," *Chicago Tribune*, December 21, 2007. www.chicagotribune.com/news/nationworld/chi-122107-ms,1,3047960.story.

Glossary

antioxidants: Chemicals that remove toxic by-products from the body known as free radicals. Foods rich in antioxidants, including many fruits and vegetables, help the body maintain its immune system.

Burkitt's lymphoma: A type of cancer found mostly in tropical climates that attacks the immune system. It is caused by the Epstein-Barr virus, which also causes infectious mononucleosis.

chronic fatigue syndrome: A mysterious disease that afflicts people with relentless fatigue, confusion, vertigo, pain, and other symptoms that can last for years. The Epstein-Barr virus is believed to be a major cause of the syndrome.

cytomegalovirus: A virus that causes about 15 percent of mono cases.

Epstein-Barr virus: A virus that causes about 85 percent of mono cases and is suspected of causing chronic fatigue syndrome, multiple sclerosis, Guillain-Barré syndrome, certain cancers, and other diseases.

hepatitis: An inflammation of the liver, often caused by mono.

herpes: A family of viruses that includes cytomegalovirus and the Epstein-Barr virus, causing a number of diseases, including mono, chicken pox, cold sores, and genital herpes.

liver: The organ in the body that stores vitamins, sugars, and fats and manufactures bile, which assists in digestion. The liver often is attacked by mono, which causes it to become enlarged.

lymph nodes: Glands that fight infection by summoning white blood cells. With mono, the lymph nodes become swollen and sore.

monocyte cells: Single-nucleus white blood cells summoned by the lymph nodes to fight viral infections that cause mononucleosis.

spleen: The organ of the body that expels old blood cells. It can become enlarged during mononucleosis.

Organizations to Contact

Chronic Fatigue and Immune Dysfunction Syndrome Association of America

PO Box 220398
Charlotte, NC 28222-0398
phone: (704) 365-2343
Web site: www.cfids.org

Founded in 1987, the organization has raised more than $22 million to support medical research into chronic fatigue syndrome. A visitor to the organization's Web site can find an overview of the disease as well as how to recognize symptoms, available treatment options, and the status of research into finding a cure.

Guillain-Barré Syndrome/Chronic Inflammatory Demyelinating Polyneuropathy Foundation International

The Holly Building
104 1/2 Forrest Ave.
Narberth, PA 19072
phone: (866) 224-3301
fax: (610) 667-7036
e-mail: info@gbsfi.com
Web site: www.gbsfi.com

The organization supports research into Guillain-Barré syndrome, which may be caused by the Epstein-Barr virus. Visitors to the organization's Web site can learn about the disease as well as chronic inflammatory demyelinating polyneuropathy, a similar disease that causes nerve damage.

Infectious Diseases Society of America

1300 Wilson Blvd., Suite 300
Arlington, VA 22209
phone: (703) 299-0200
fax: (703) 299-0204
Web site: www.idsociety.org

The Infectious Diseases Society of America represents physicians, scientists, and other health-care professionals who study and treat infectious diseases. Visitors to the organization's Web site can find many resources about mononucleosis, including news articles about scientific advancements as well as graphs and illustrations about the disease and its prevalence in American society.

National Institutes of Health

9000 Rockville Pike
Bethesda, MD 20892
phone: (301) 496-4000
e-mail: NIHinfo@od.nih.gov
Web site: www.nih.gov

The National Institutes of Health is the chief funding arm of the federal government for medical research. Many resources about infectious mononucleosis are available on the agency's Web site, including an overview of the symptoms, an explanation of the monospot test, and options for treatment.

National Multiple Sclerosis Society

733 Third Ave., 3rd Fl.
New York, NY 10017

phone: (800) 344-4867

Web site: www.nationalmssociety.org

Medical research has recently identified the Epstein-Barr virus as a possible cause for multiple sclerosis (MS), a severe
disease that damages nerves and often robs patients of their
ability to walk. The society provides support to MS sufferers
and funds research into the causes and cures. Visitors to the
society's Web site can find many resources about MS, including recent news stories about the disease and strategies for
treating patients.

U.S. Centers for Disease Control and Prevention

Office of Communication

Building 16, D-42

1600 Clifton Rd., NE

Atlanta, GA 30333

phone: (800) 311-3435

e-mail: cdcinfo@cdc.gov

Web site: www.cdc.gov

The federal government's chief public health agency
explores trends in diseases and other conditions that
affect the health of Americans. Visitors to the agency's
Web site can find pages devoted to the Epstein-Barr virus, which is regarded as a primary cause of infectious
mononucleosis.

World Health Organization (WHO)

Avenue Appia 20

CH-1211 Geneva 27

Switzerland

phone: 41-22-791-2111

fax: 41-22-791-3111

e-mail: info@who.int
Web site: www.who.int/en

WHO is the public health arm of the United Nations. WHO's Web site offers many resources on the Epstein-Barr virus and how it affects people in developing countries who are susceptible to Burkitt's lymphoma.

For Further Reading

Books

Roberto Patarca-Montero, *Treatment of Chronic Fatigue Syndrome in the Antiviral Revolution Era*. Binghamton, NY: Haworth, 2001. This book argues that the Epstein-Barr virus is at the root of chronic fatigue syndrome and explains some of the drug therapies under study that could help wipe out EBV-related diseases, including infectious mononucleosis.

Matthew Paul Turner, *Everything You Need to Know Before College: A Student's Survival Guide*. Colorado Springs: NavPress, 2006. Written for students preparing to leave home for college, this book includes a chapter on wellness and how to avoid diseases that spread through dormitories.

James E. Williams, *Viral Immunity*. Charlottesville, VA: Hampton Roads, 2007. This book includes a comprehensive overview of viral infections, including infectious mononucleosis, and strategies for avoiding them. The author keeps medical terms to a minimum and urges employing natural methods such as reducing stress and eating foods rich in antioxidants as the best strategy for building up immunity against viral infections.

Periodicals

Larry Katzenstein, "Betting on Seabiscuit," *Smithsonian*, December 2002. This article chronicles the life of Laura Hillenbrand, who overcame chronic fatigue syndrome to write *Seabiscuit: An American Legend*.

Lisa Liddane, "Higher Education Involves Taking Charge of Your Wellness," *Orange County Register*, September 6, 2006. The newspaper's medical columnist provides advice for students on how to establish good personal hygiene, maintain a healthy immunity, and avoid infectious diseases.

Alice Park, "When Bad Bugs Go Good," *Time*, March 28, 2005. This article provides an overview of the research into altering the genetic makeup of viruses as a method of wiping out the Epstein-Barr virus and other diseases.

Kirsten Weir, "Oh, No! Mono," *Current Health 2*, September 2005. This article provides basic information on the disease, how it is spread, and what can be done to minimize the symptoms.

Janet Farrar Worthington, "A Healthy Student Body," *Careers and Colleges*, March/April 2005. This article provides tips on avoiding the "freshman fifteen" while suggesting ways to build up immunity against disease and otherwise maintain good personal hygiene.

Internet Sources

Michael Deichen, "Fall Illness and Hand Hygiene," September 26, 2007. http://ucfhealthservices.blogspot.com.

Elizabeth Somers, "College Freshmen Can Avoid the 'Freshman 15,'" CNN.com, August 19, 1999. www.cnn.com/HEALTH/diet.fitness/9908/19/freshman.fifteen.

Brandee J. Tecson, "LFO Singer Rich Cronin Hospitalized with Leukemia," MTV News, April 14, 2005. www.mtv.com/news/articles/1500203/20050414/lfo.jhtml.

Web Sites

American Experience, **The Boy in the Bubble** (www.pbs.org/wgbh/amex/bubble/gallery/index.html). This is the companion Web site to the 2006 PBS *American Experience* documentary about David Vetter, the boy who was forced to live in a plastic bubble because his body lacked natural immunity.

Diet, Exercise, Stress, and the Immune System (www.cleve landclinic.org/health/health-info/docs/0900/0955.asp?index=5429). This noted clinic based in Cleveland, Ohio, has provided a comprehensive guide to maintaining a healthy immune system through eating antioxidant-rich foods, exercising regularly, and reducing stress.

Epstein-Barr Virus and Infectious Mononucleosis (www. cdc.gov/ncidod/diseases/ebv.htm). Maintained by the U.S. Centers for Disease Control and Prevention, this Web site provides an overview of infectious mononucleosis and the virus that causes most of the cases. The site also explains the monospot test, which is the primary blood test used to diagnose mono.

Mononucleosis (www.mayoclinic.com/health/mononucleosis/DS00352). The Mayo Clinic, which is one of the nation's leading research hospitals, provides a thorough background on infectious mononucleosis and discusses some of the complications, including meningitis, anemia, and obstructed breathing.

Viral Cancers (www.who.int/vaccine_research/diseases/viral_cancers/en/index1.html). The World Health Organization, which is the public health arm of the United Nations, discusses the Epstein-Barr virus and how it causes certain cancers, including Burkitt's lymphoma and nasopharyngeal carcinoma.

Index

Picture Credits

About the Author

Hal Marcovitz has written more than one hundred books for young readers. His other title in the Diseases and Disorders series is *Blindness*. A former newspaper reporter, he lives in Chalfont, Pennsylvania, with his wife, Gail, and daughters, Michelle and Ashley.